Erstwhile Friends
AND SIMPLER DAYS

A Photographic Retrospective

J.C. Leatherman

with Lyndell Leatherman

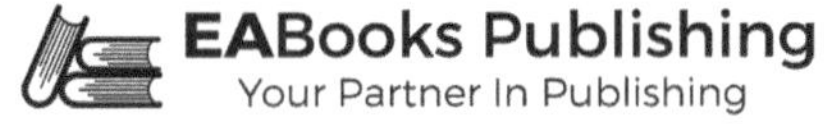

EABooks Publishing
Your Partner In Publishing

Cover design: Robin Black
Cover photo: Mark Murphy
Back cover photo: iStockphoto, Bernhard Jaeck
Author photo: Lyndell Leatherman, Kansas City, Missouri, 2024 (Bob Stewart)

ISBN: 978-1-963611-52-6
LCCN: 2024916552

Published by EA Books Publishing, a division of
Living Parables of Central Florida, Inc. a 501c3
EABooksPublishing.com

Contents

Foreword

The author of these poems, Jack Clinton (J.C.) Leatherman, was born in 1927 in Lamar, Missouri. His parents, Harry and Edith, like many others during the Great Depression, lost their homestead . . . and so were forced to rent farms from there on out. Like so many of their generation, they scratched out a living through honest labor and fair dealings with their neighbors. Their four children—Alice, Pauline, Oliver (Bud), and Jack–learned a healthy work ethic guided by Christian principles and an appreciation for our country's freedoms and opportunities.

Jack was uncommonly studious, as demonstrated by his memorization of many poems which he could still quote into adulthood, e.g., "Thanatopsis," "Stopping by the Woods on a Snowy Evening," "The Charge of the Light Brigade," and "If." The photo at right shows Jack (top row, right end) and his 11-year-old classmates at Belmont School, Vernon County, Missouri. According to family lore, he owned just

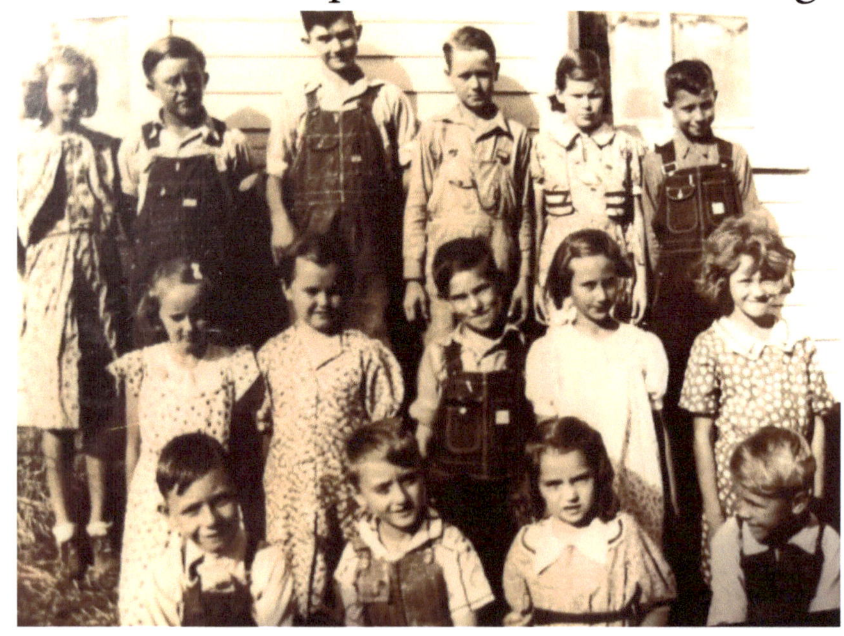

Belmont School, Vernon County, Missouri, 1938, photographer unknown

two pairs of overalls at any given time—the newer for church and school and the older for work.

Following graduation from Lamar High School, Jack attended God's Bible School in Cincinnati, Ohio, where he met his future wife, Wilma, a musically-talented English major from southeast Ohio. Upon completing their studies in 1950, they entered 42 years of ministry–pastoring churches in Baxter Springs, Kansas; Joplin, Missouri; and Green Rock (now Colona), Eureka, Milan, and Macomb, Illinois. Along the way, they raised four children–Lyndell, David, Phillip, and Mary Beth.

Jack never forgot his humble roots and occasionally channeled his nostalgia into writing poems–four of which comprise the volume you are now holding. Sadly, he left us far too soon, passing suddenly in 1993. But his godly legacy lives on in his descendants and the lives of hundreds touched by his ministry and good humor. (Though he tried to look serious for this photo shoot, his default demeanor was much more jovial, as anyone who knew him can attest).

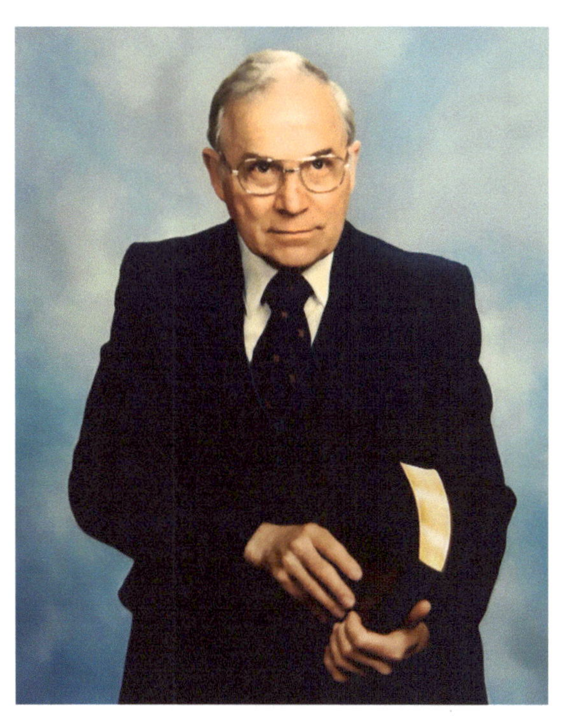

photographer unknown

We miss you, Dad, but thanks for these poems to remember you by. Speaking of poems, here's one (actually a song lyric) that I wrote in your honor while driving back to Illinois on the morning I received word of your passing:

Single heart, single mind,
Seeking first the kingdom,
Pressing toward the prize that waits
For those who run the race.
Single aim, single goal:
Loving people, winning souls.
Undivided loyalty
To Christ the risen Lord.

And a life lived for Jesus
Is an offering that pleases
The Father above,
The Father of Love.
Finding by losing,
Living by choosing
Treasures above
That don't fade away,
Won't fade away,
Treasures that don't fade away.

Lyndell Leatherman
Harrisonville, Missouri

I.

LONELY CASTLES

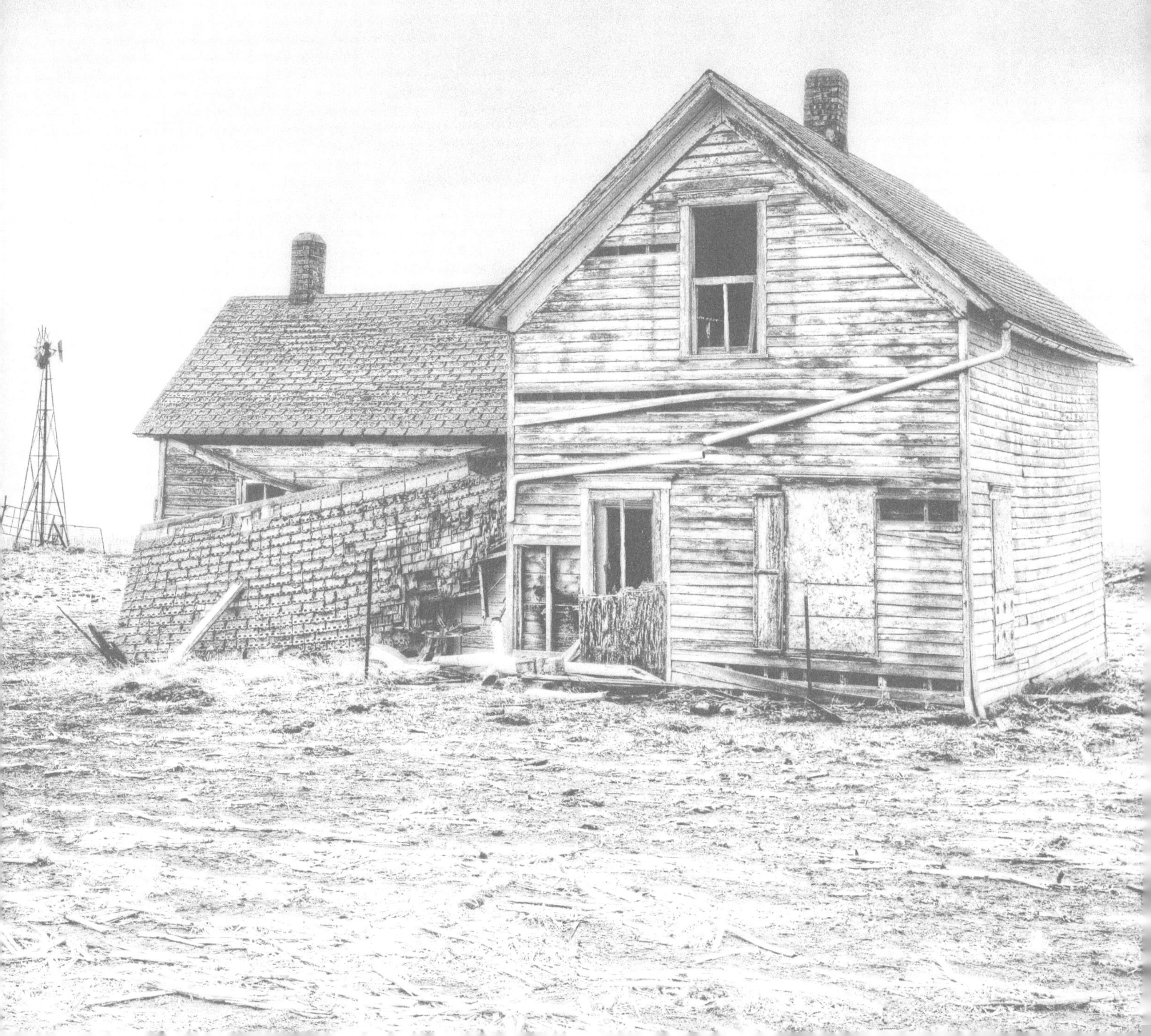

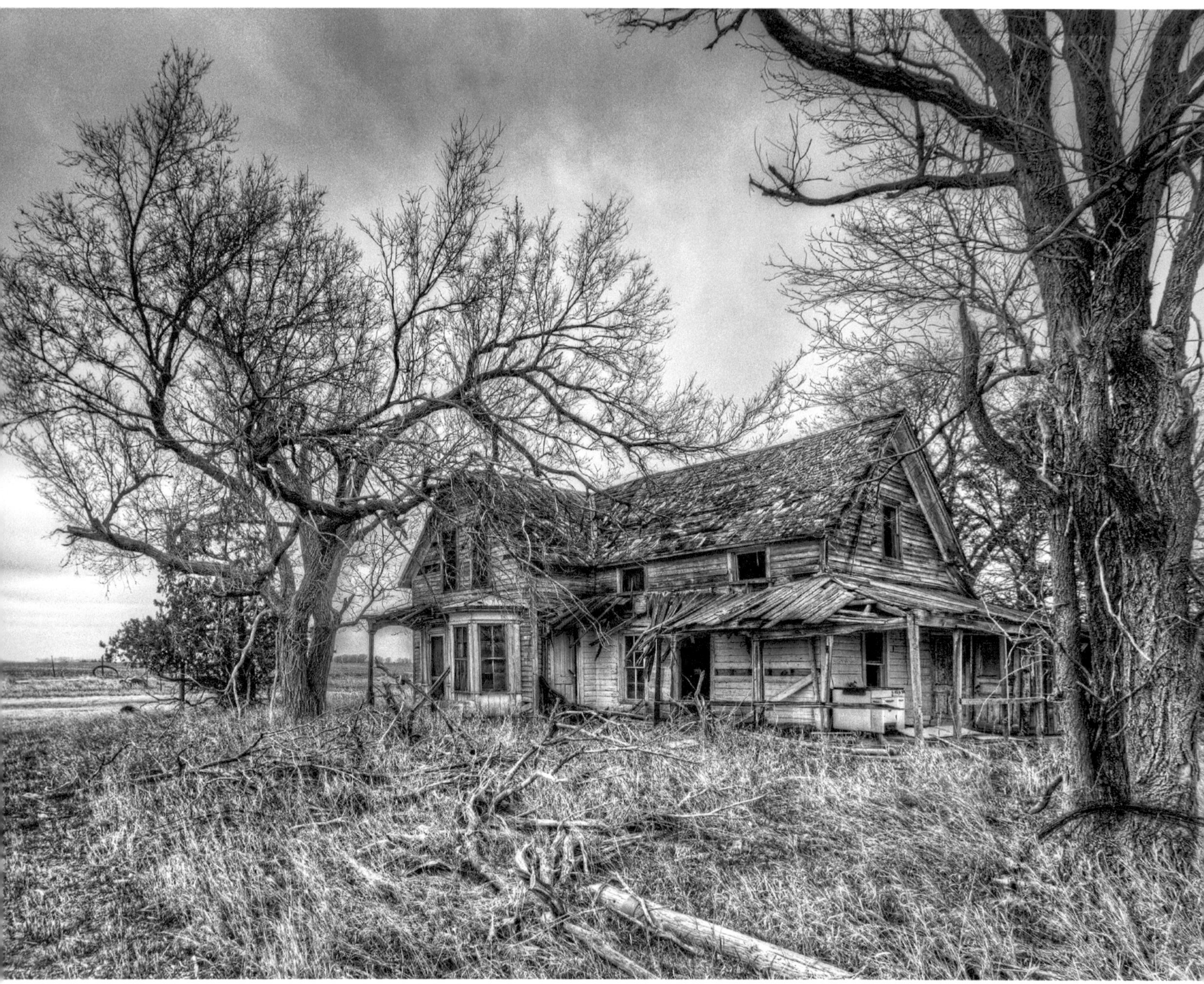

Ghost house, Cawker City, Kansas (Dave McKane)

I seldom pass abandoned homes
Without a wistful sort of twinge;

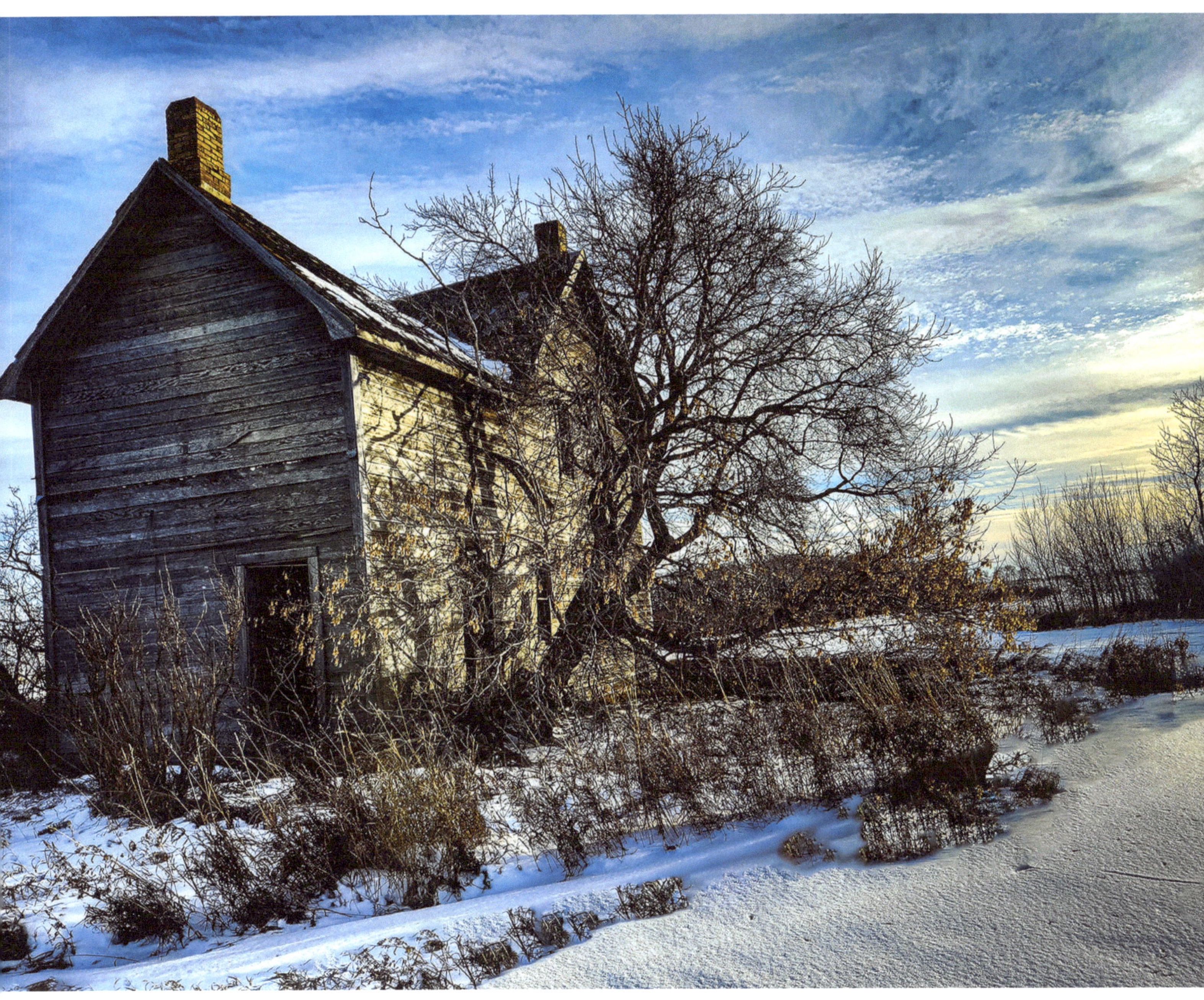

Winter farmhouse, Saskatchewan (Cris Sia Moresca):

Beneath those roofs, within those walls,

The sagas of a nation hinge.

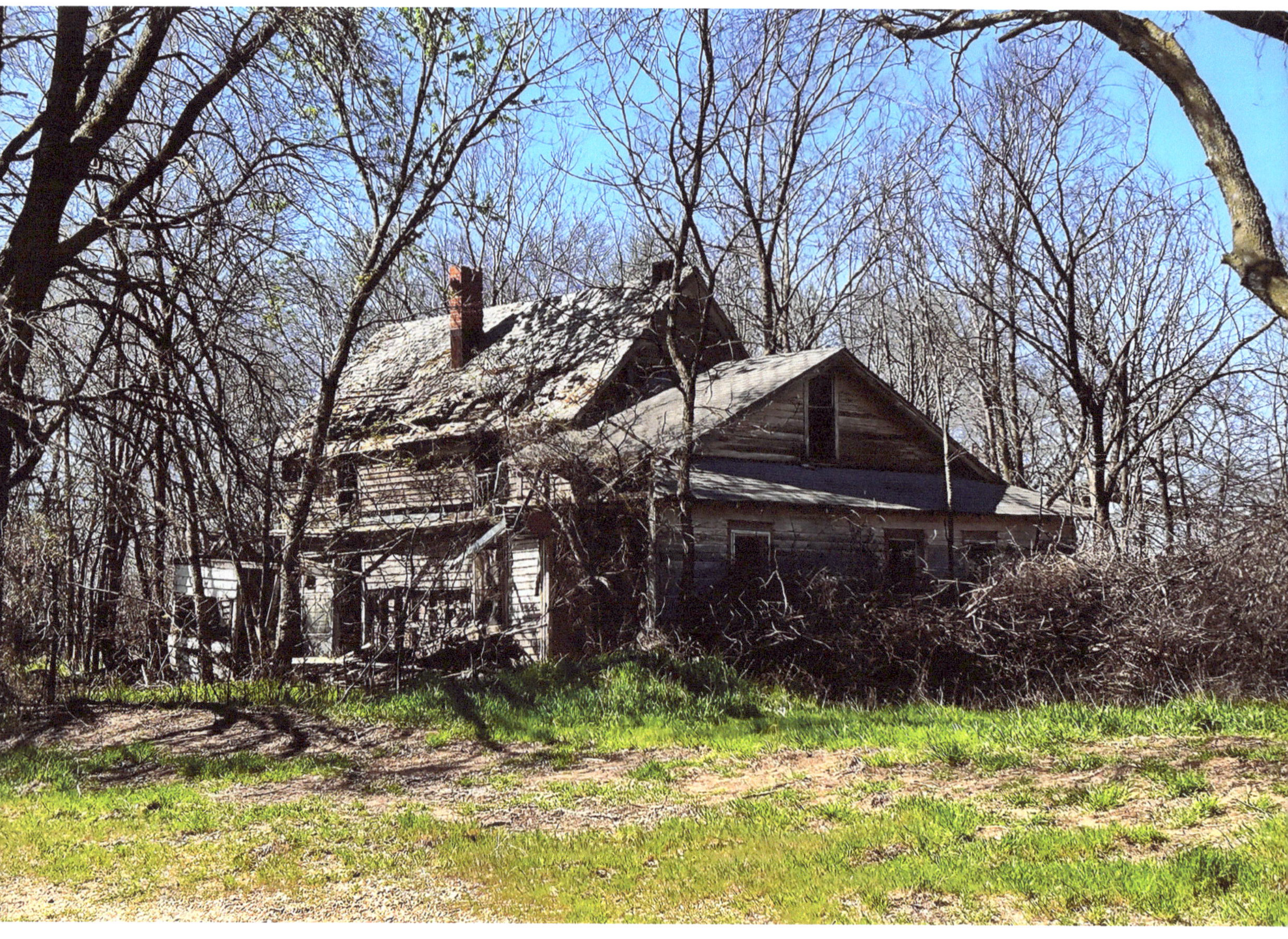

Crumbling house, Kansas (Mark Pendergrass)

Each tells a story of its own.

Now take that house beneath the hill:

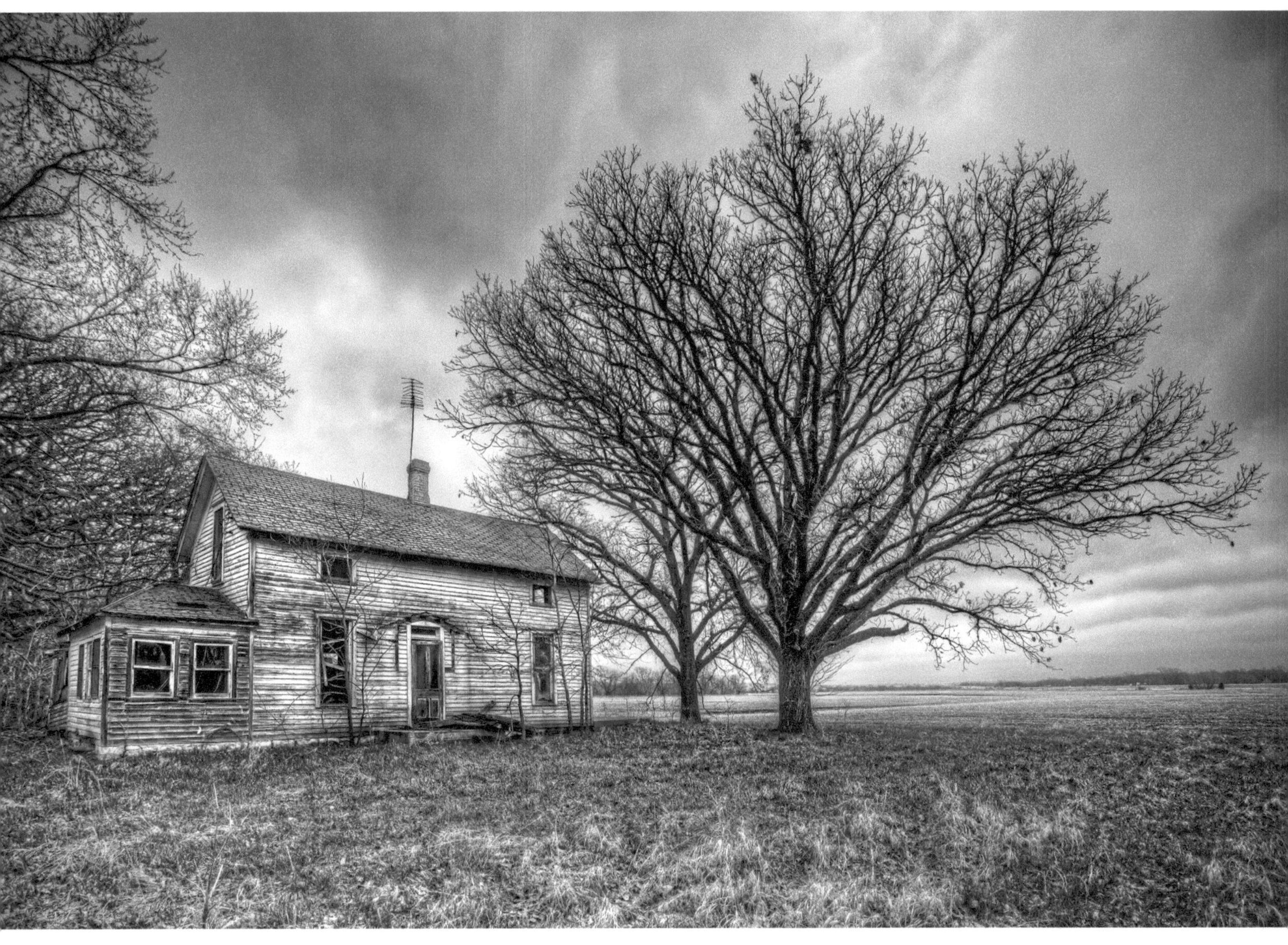

Ghost house, Cedar Point #4, Kansas (Dave McKane)

One year a father helped his son
Erect it there with care and skill.

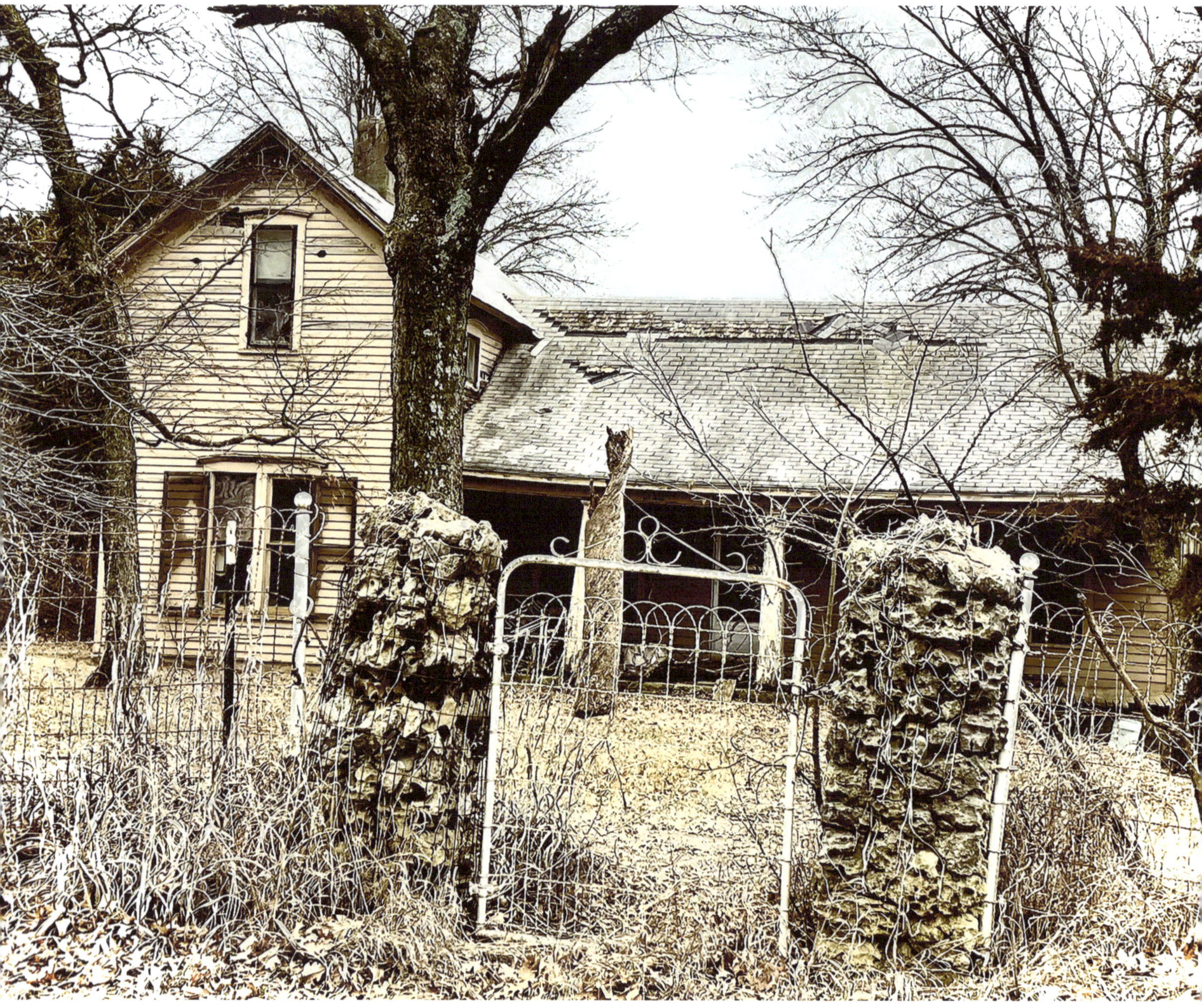

Farmhouse and gate, Kansas (Mark Pendergrass)

The son then brought his lovely bride
And carried her across the sill;

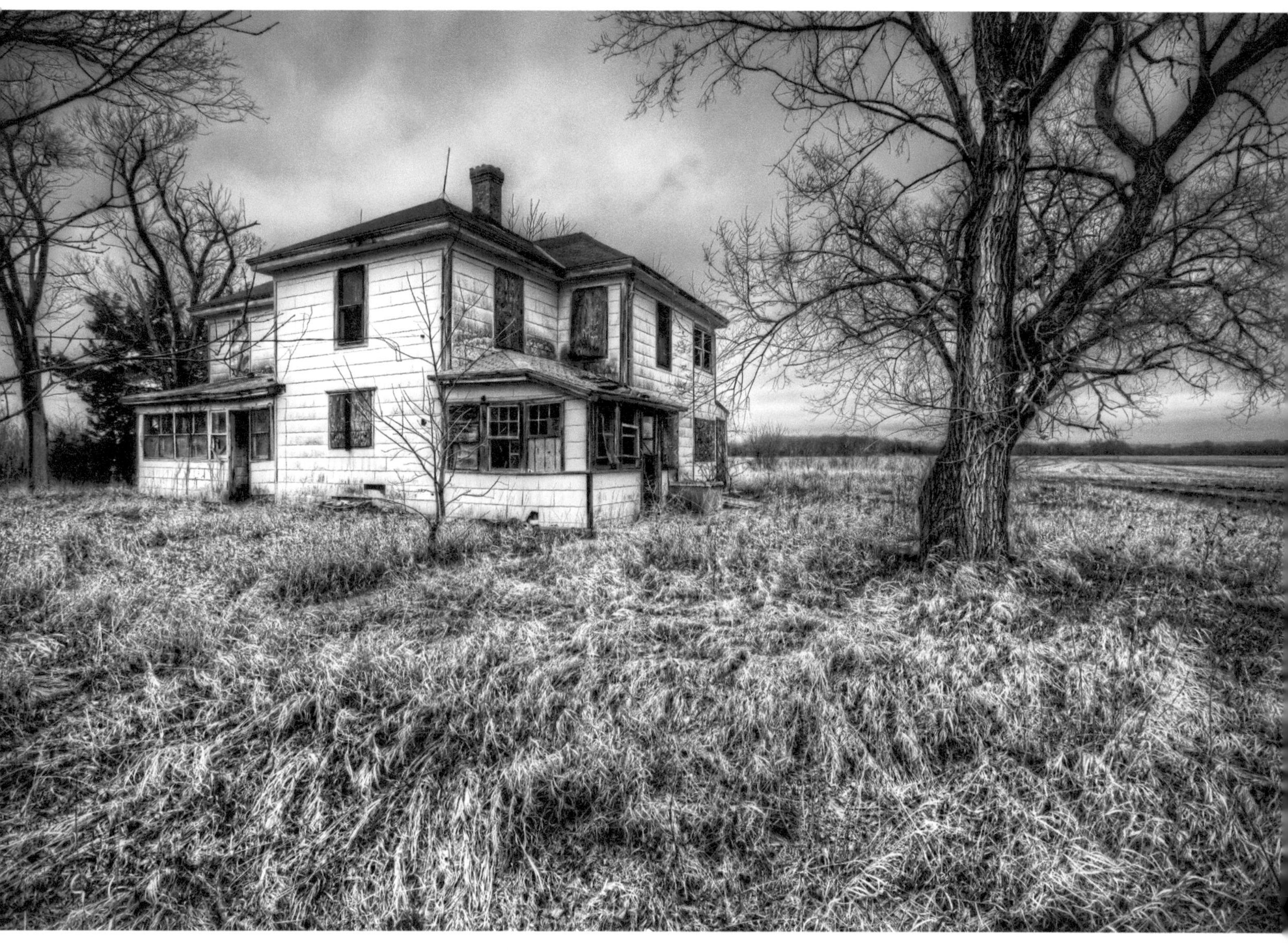

Ghost house, Clements, Kansas (Dave McKane)

Then many happy years went by
And offspring came, their lives to fill.

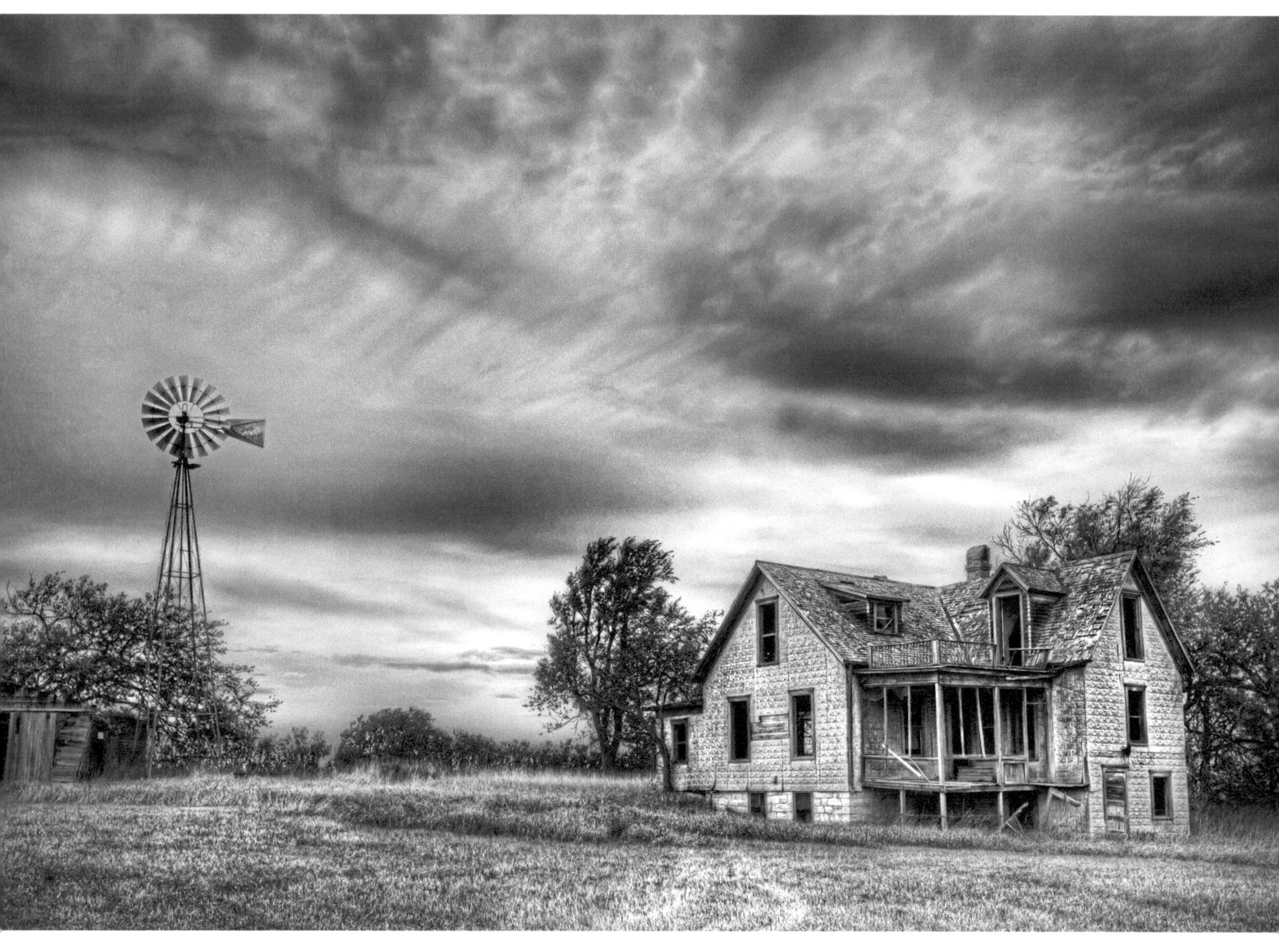

Ghost house, Ellsworth #1, Kansas (Dave McKane)

Ofttimes the sound of laughter sweet
Did echo through this homey place;

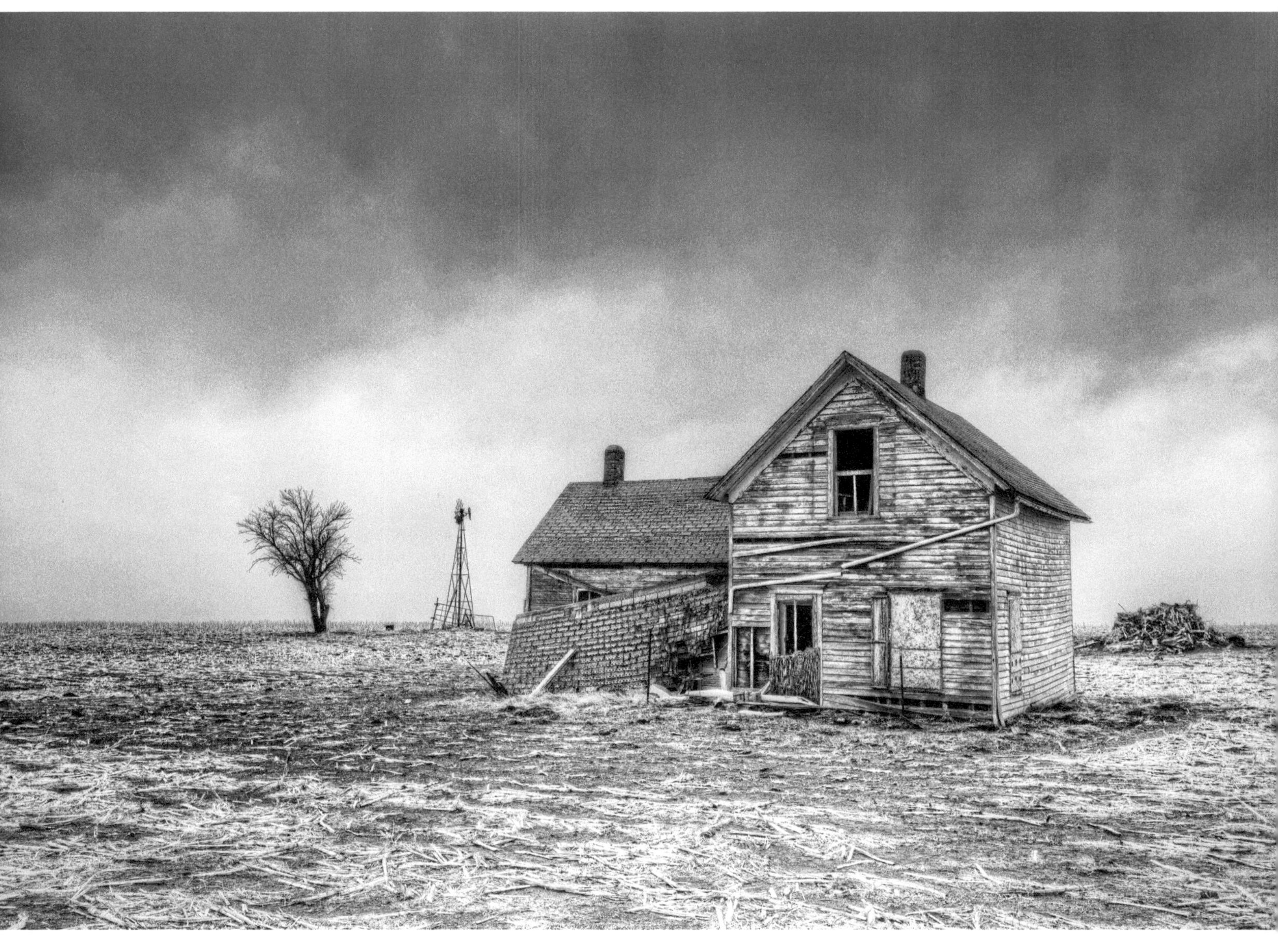

Ghost house, Clements #2, Kansas (Dave McKane)

And children's hurts were quickly eased
By mother's love and gentle grace.

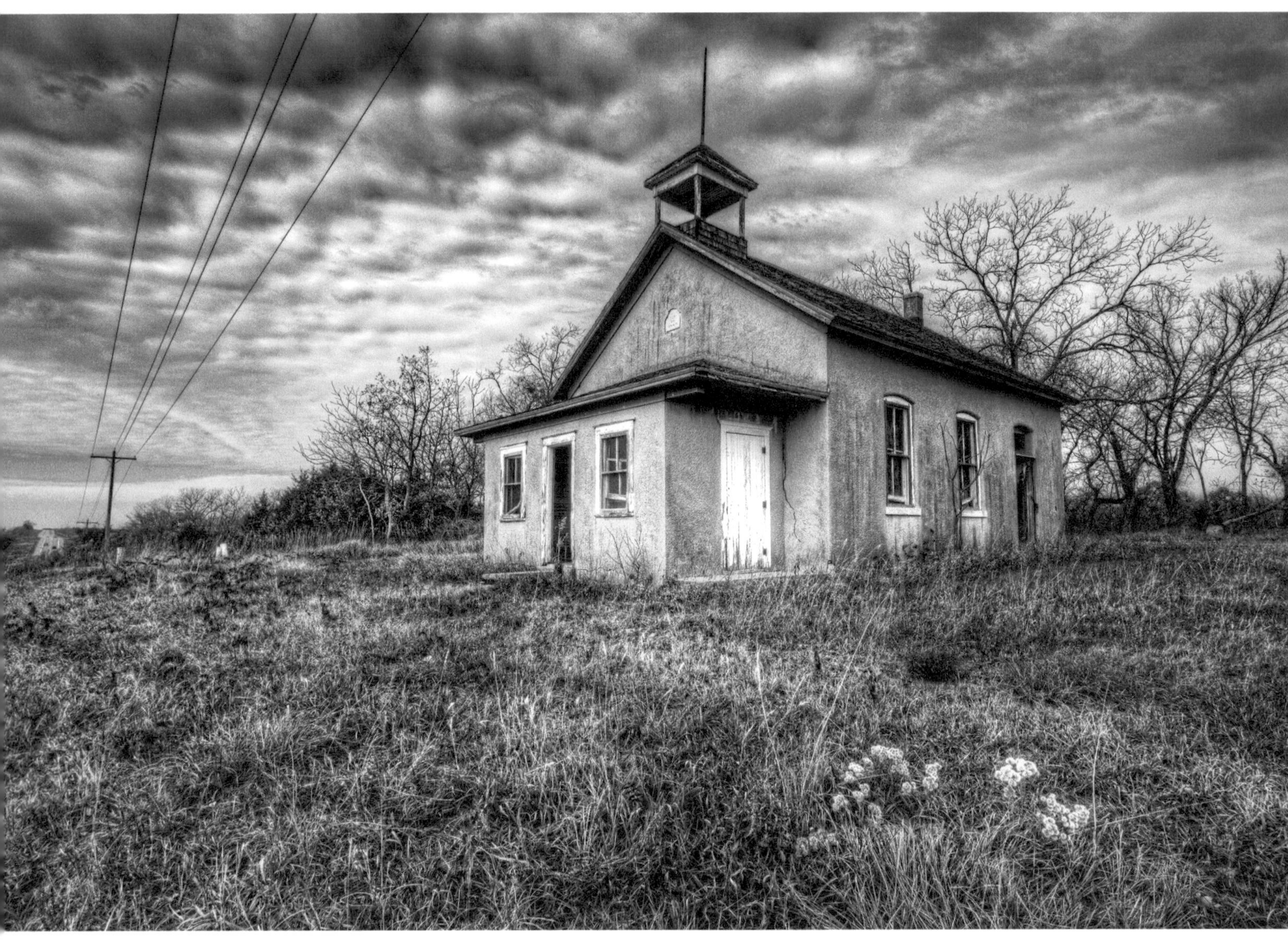

Ghost house, Lecompton, Kansas (Dave McKane)

Her young'ns grew, skipped off to school,
Came home to scent of bread, fresh baked;

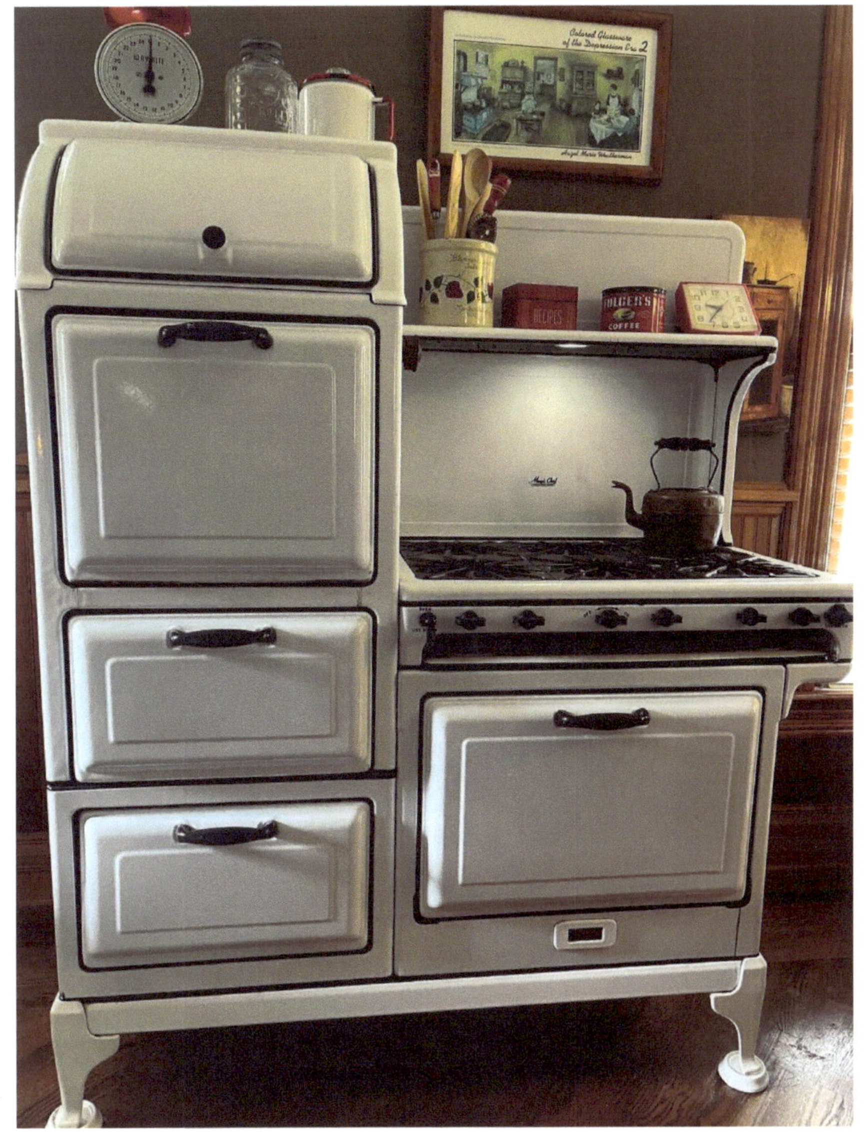

Magic Chef stove, Harrisonville, Missouri 2024
(Lyndell Leatherman)

The chores were done, and supper served,
Where hearty appetites were slaked.

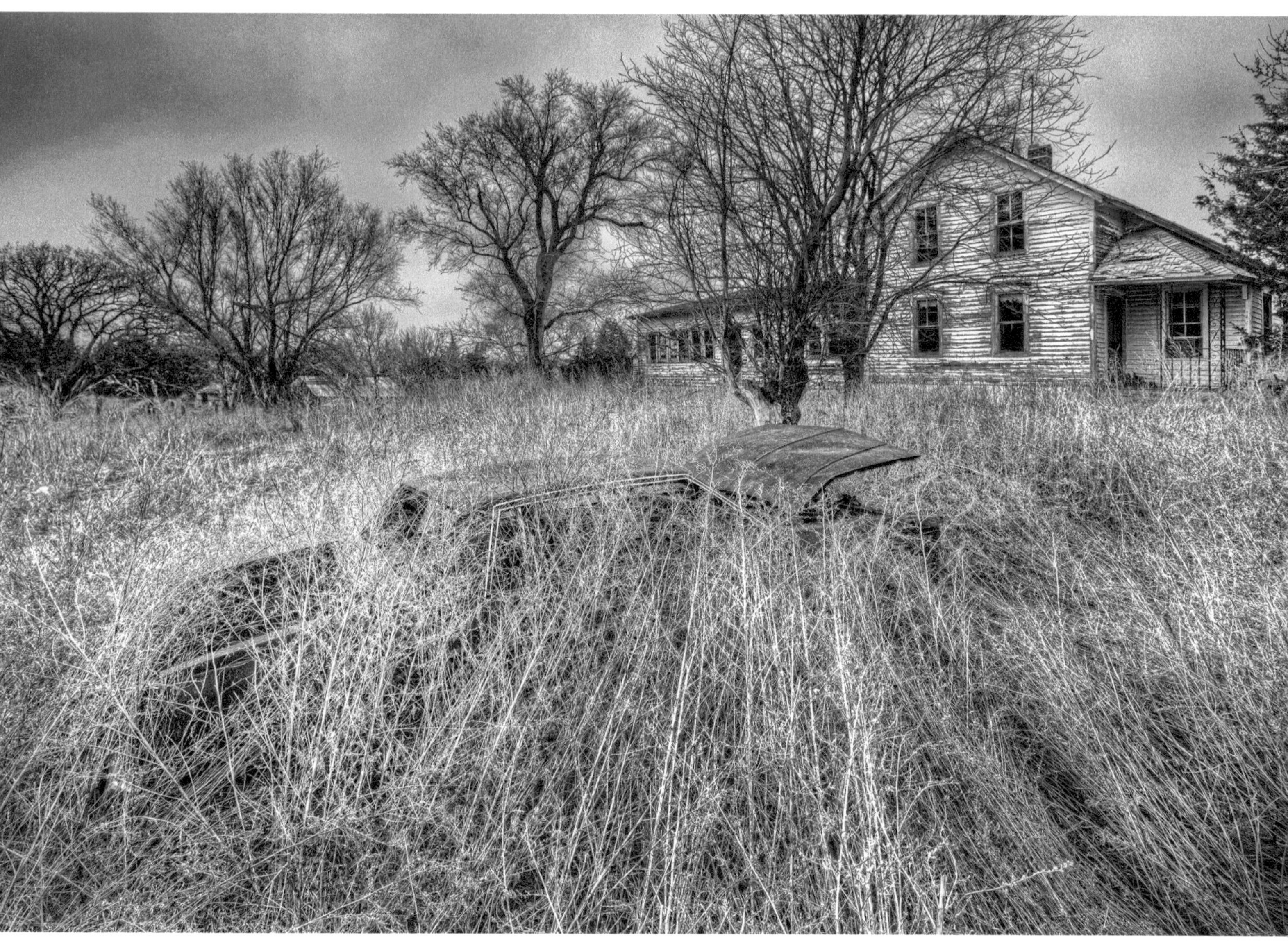

Ghost house, Downs #2, Kansas (Dave McKane)

Then all too soon the kids were grown;
Some journeyed east, and others west

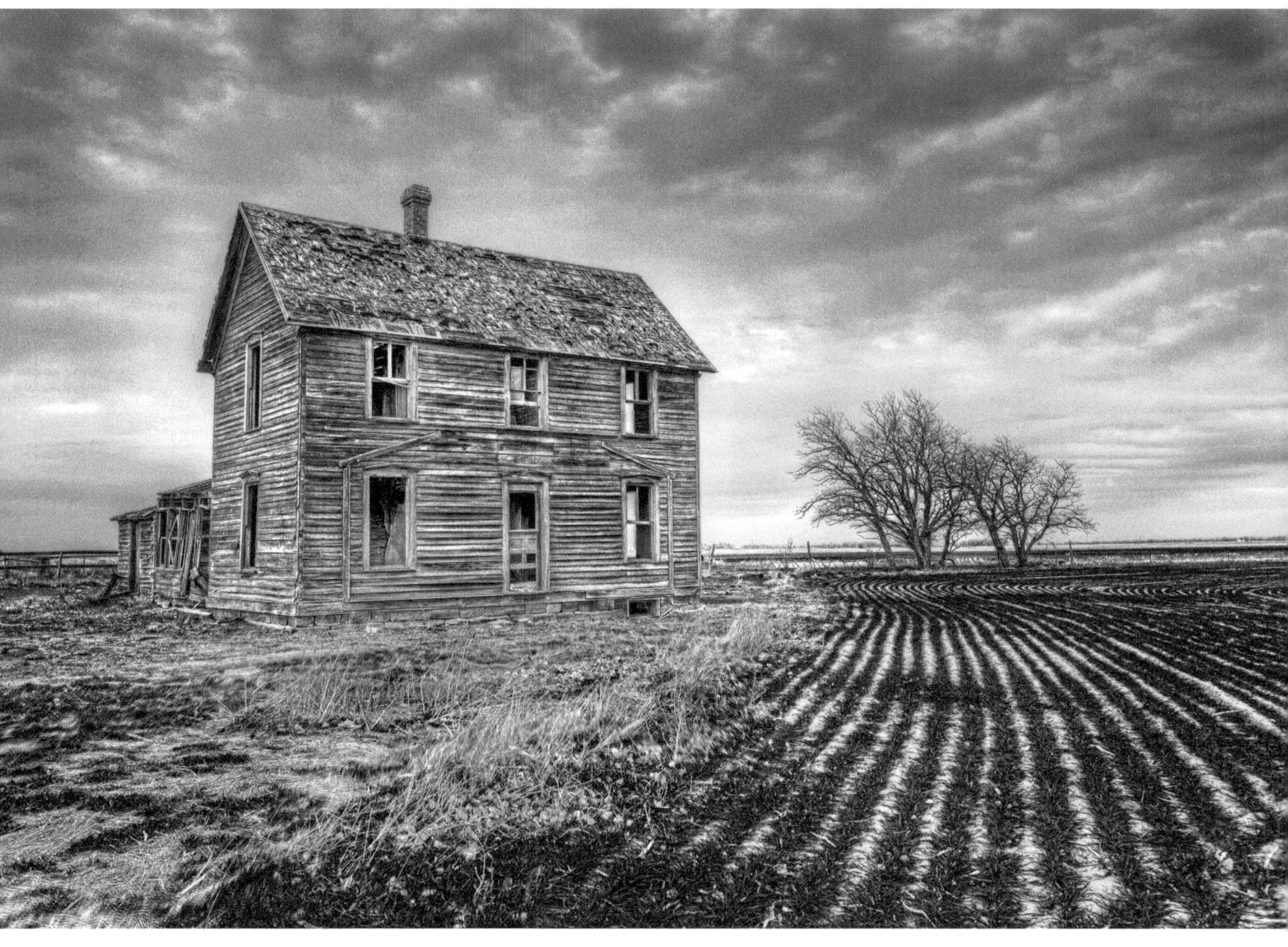

Ghost house, Dodge City #1, Kansas (Dave McKane)

To seek careers in distant towns.
The home became an empty nest.

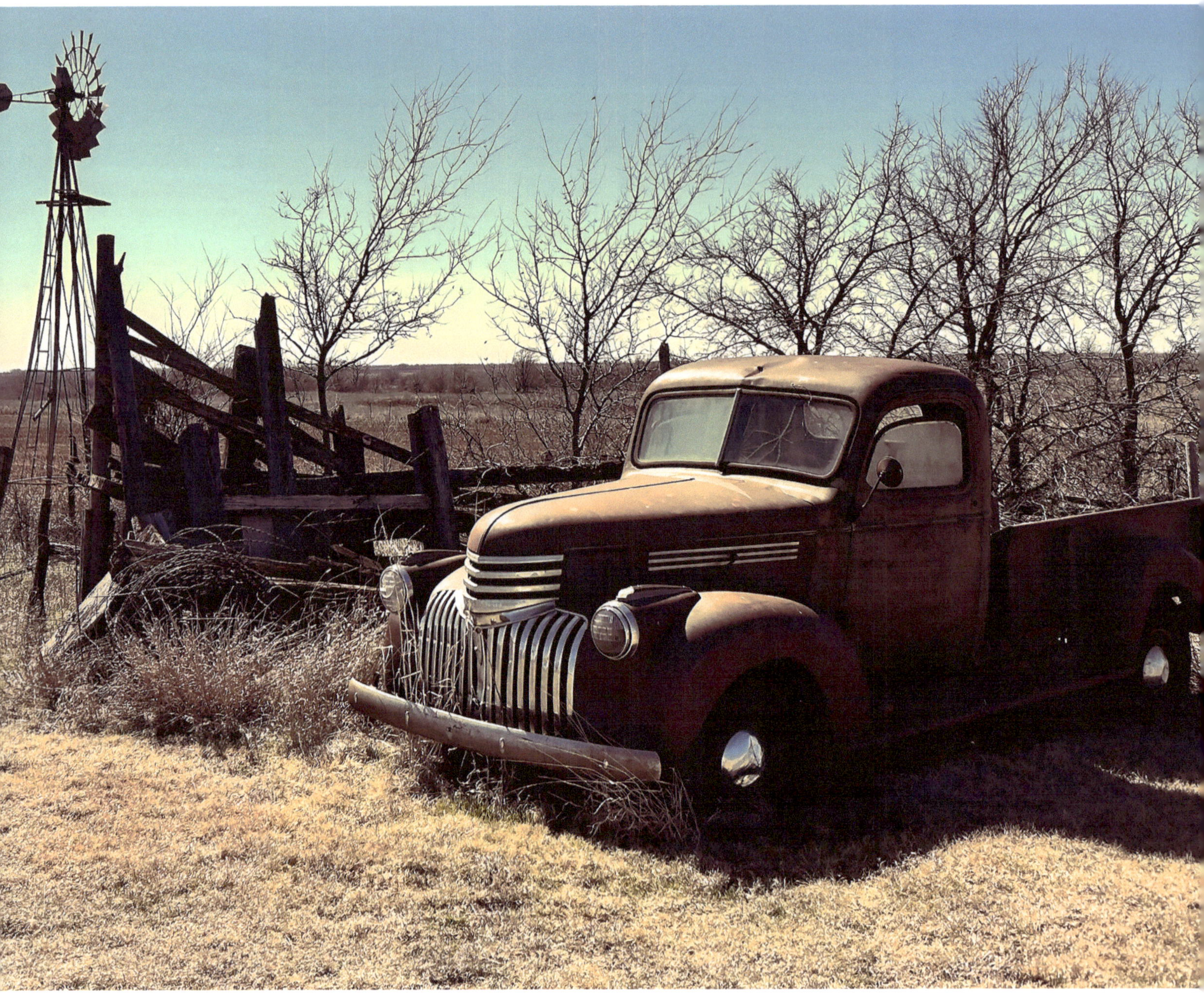

Abandoned truck, Kansas (Mark Pendergrass)

It soon declined for want of care,
The parents too, with passing years.

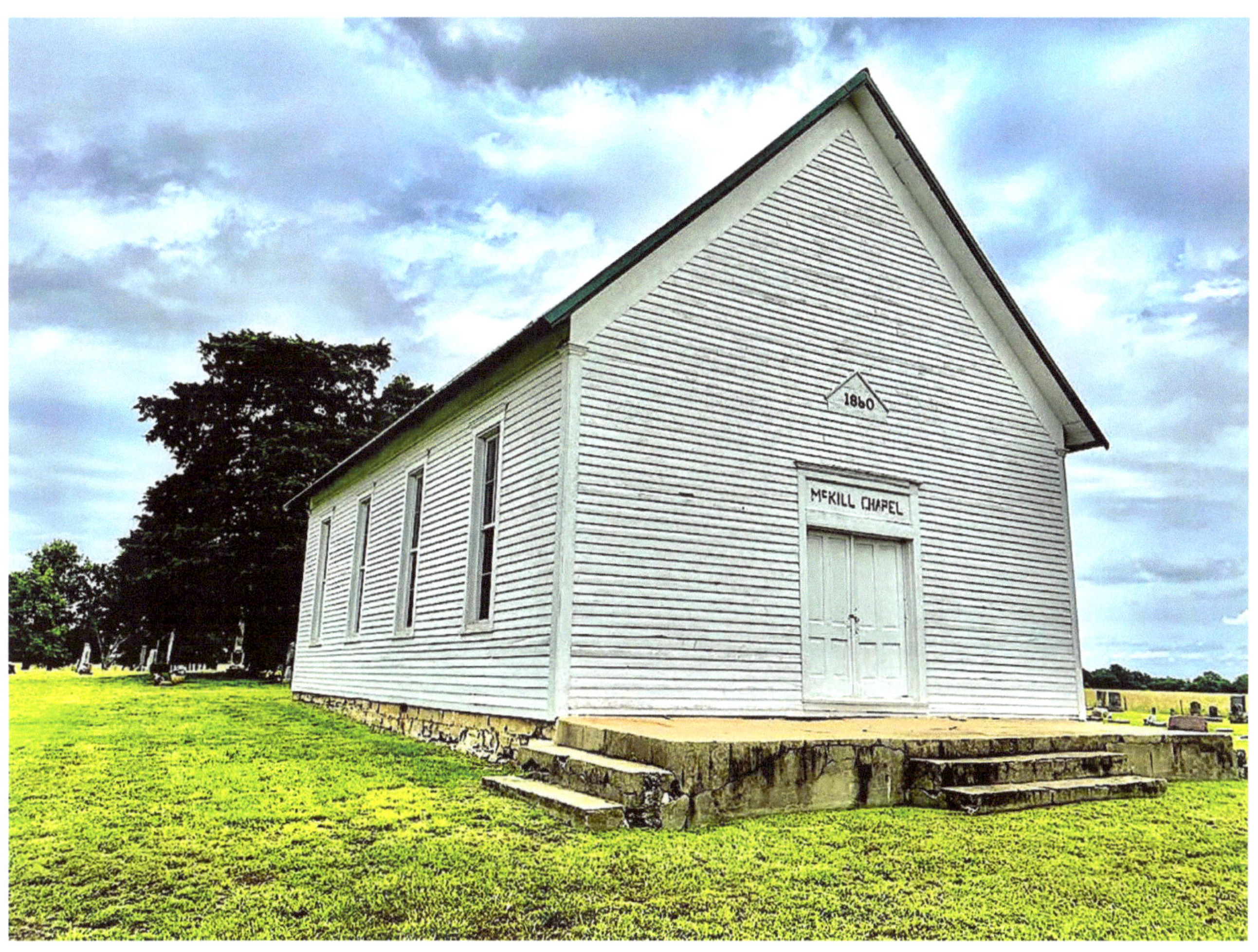

McKill Chapel, Vernon County, Missouri, 2024 (Lyndell Leatherman)

And each, in turn, at the old church yard,
Was bid farewell through falling tears.

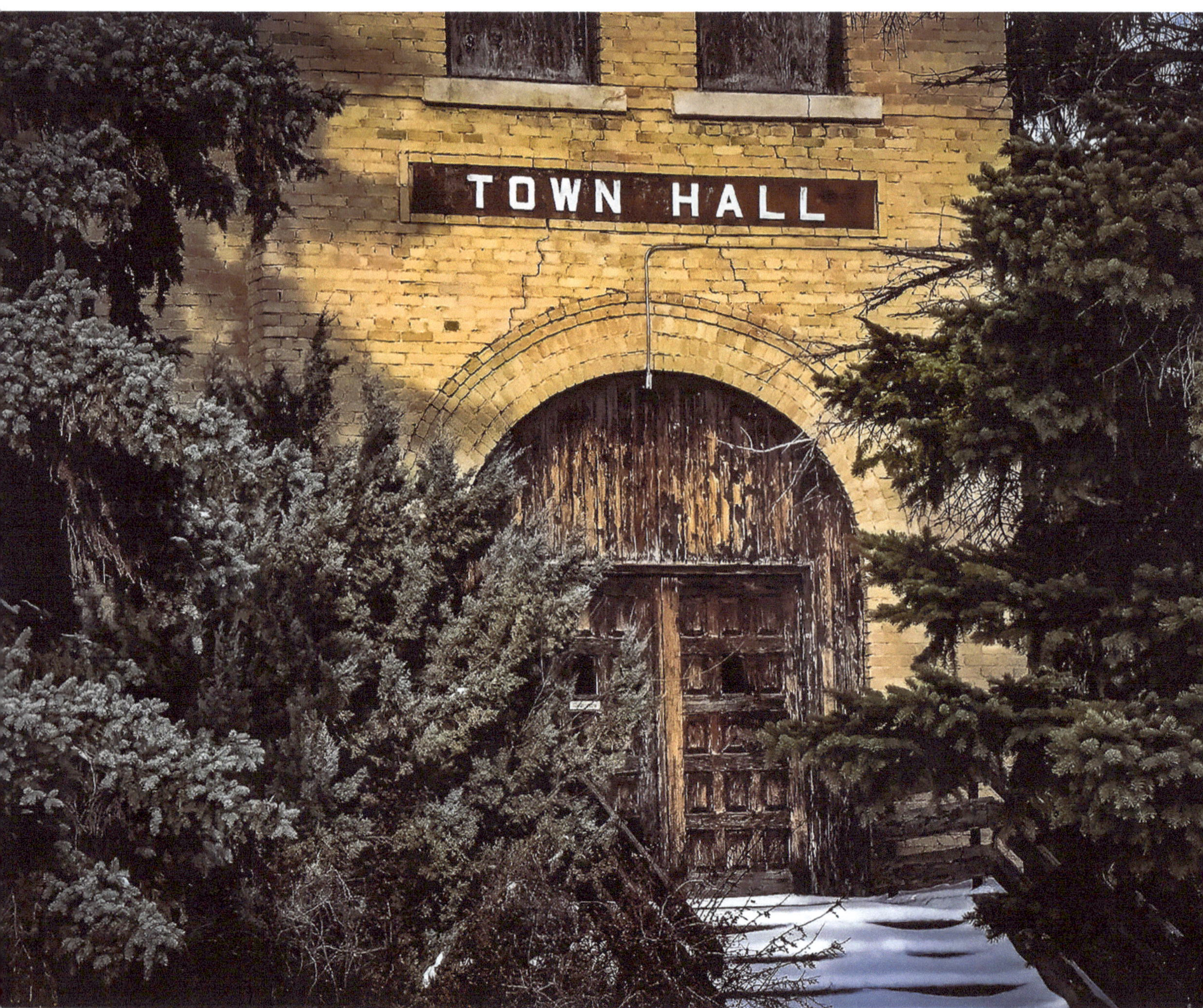

Town Hall, Claybank, Saskatchewan (Cris Sia Moresca)

A family conference was called;
The neighbor asked to rent the farm.

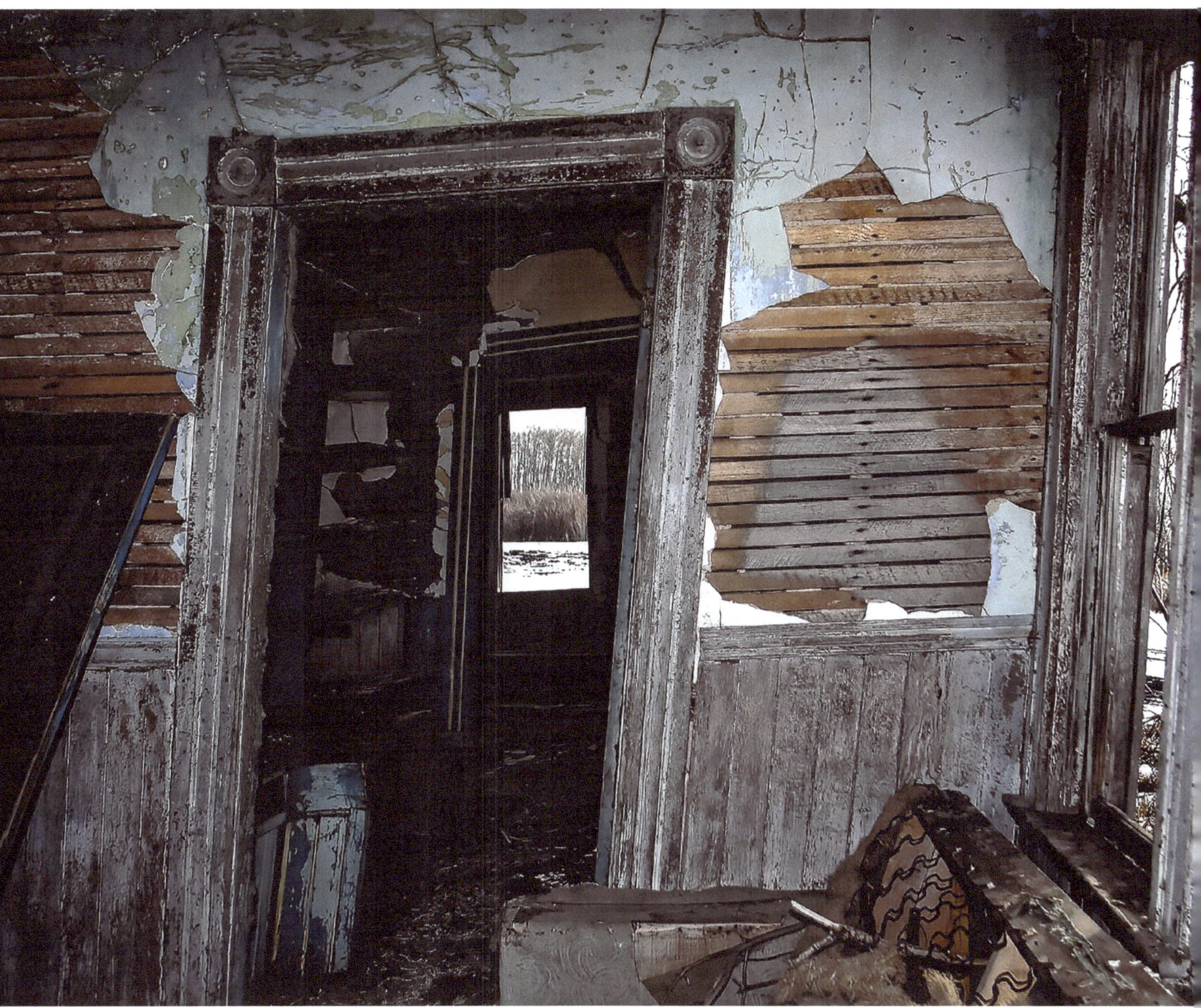

. Interior damage, Saskatchewan (Cris Sia Moresca)

But no one seemed to want the house;

To fix 'er up would cost an arm.

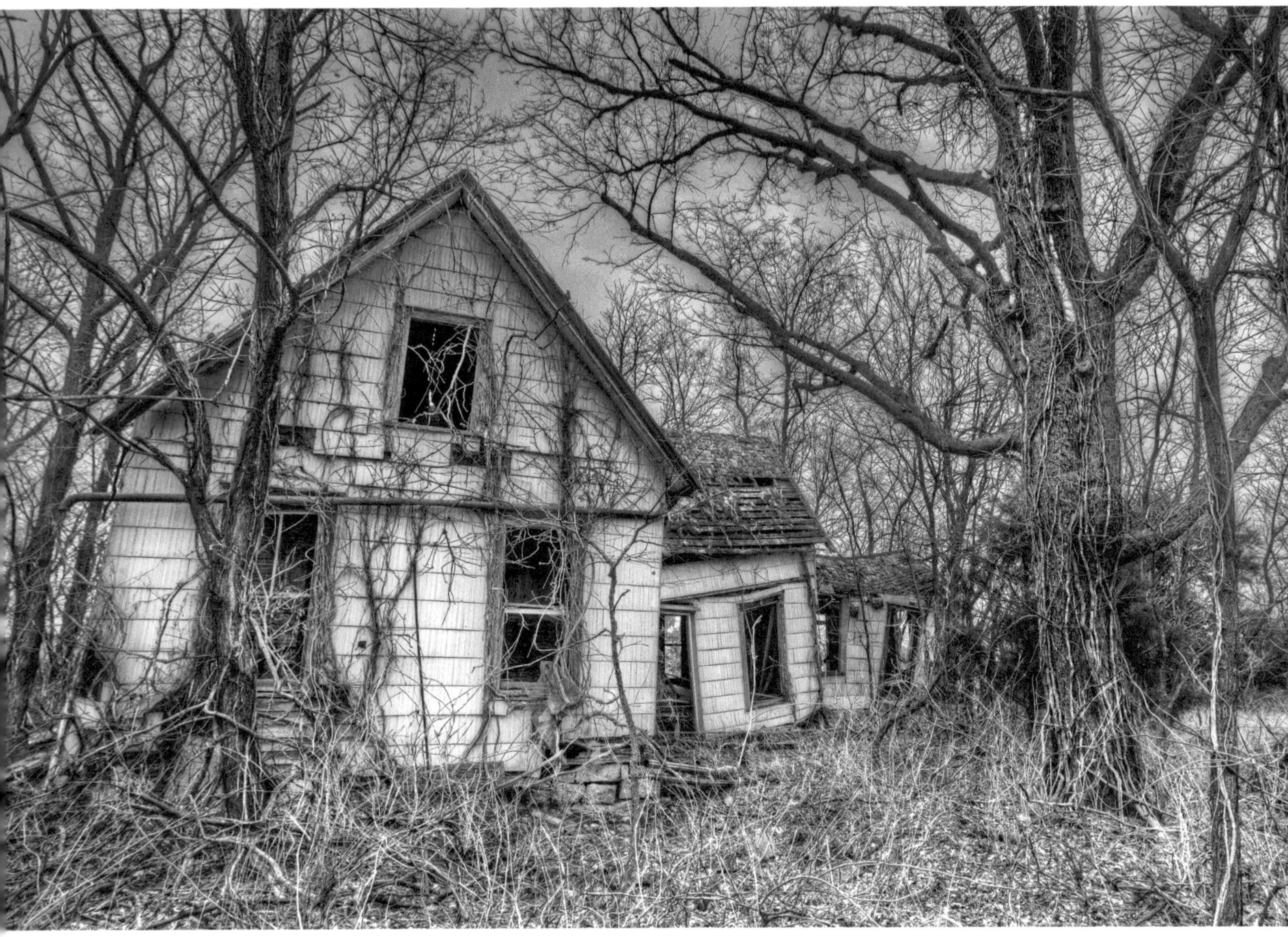

Ghost house, Paola #3, Kansas (Dave McKane)

Forthwith the place was left to fate,
And nature worked its havoc well:

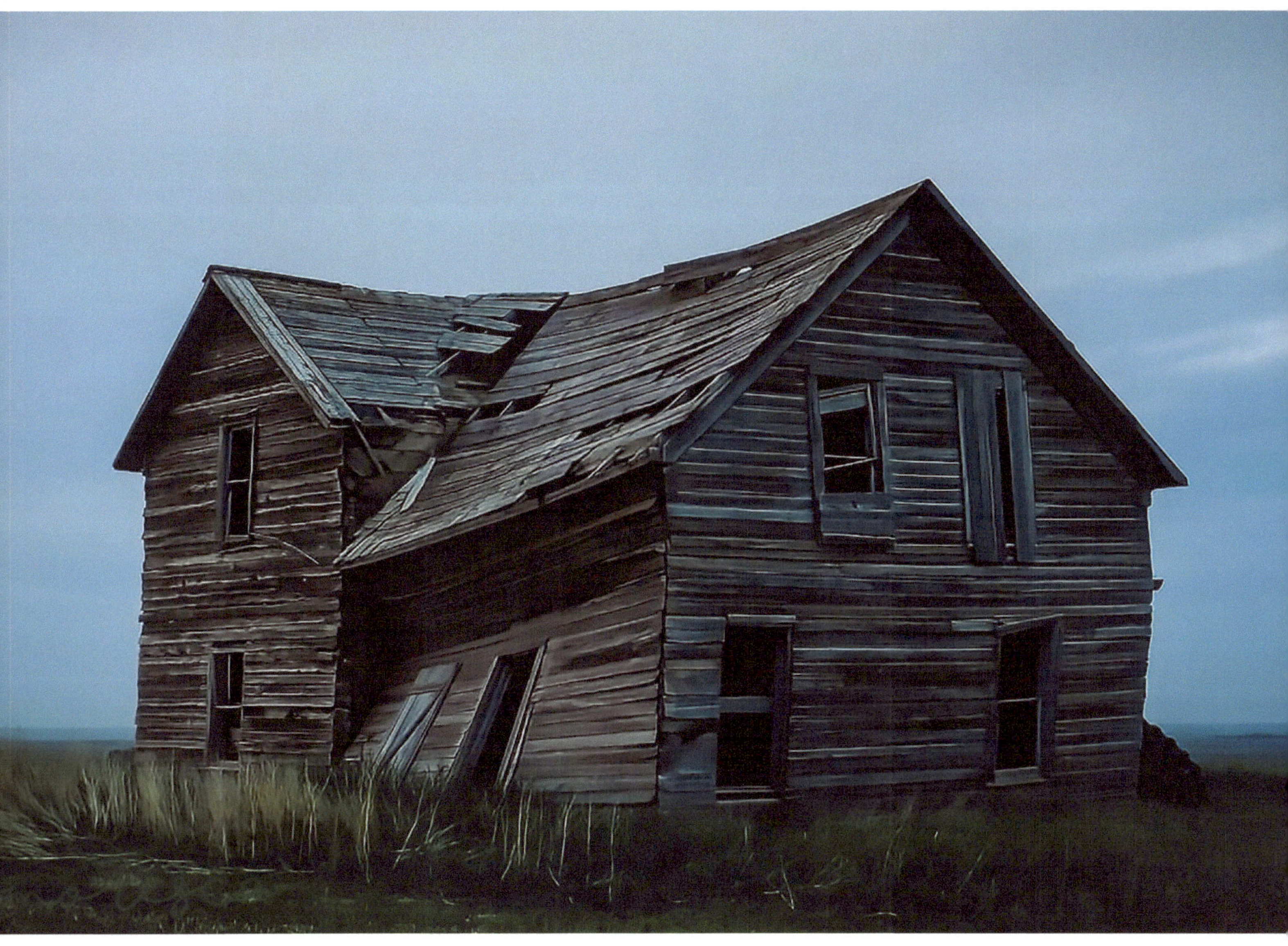

Collapsing house, Ogema, Saskatchewan (Cris Sia Moresca)

The glass would break, the paint would peel,
And shingles flew as winds would swell.

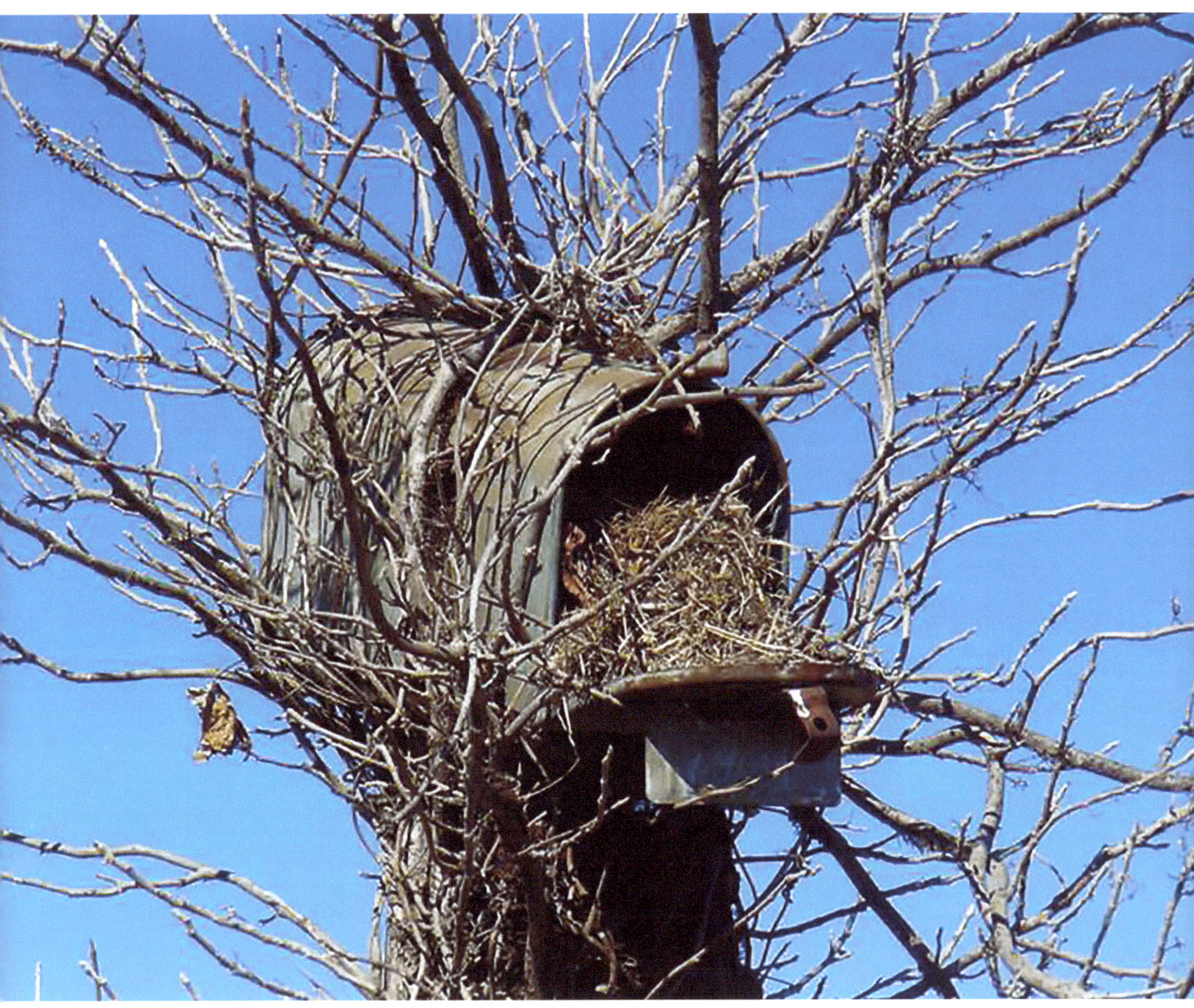

Nest in mailbox, Kansas (Mark Pendergrass)

The animals, both winged and furred,
Found haven in its littered shell.

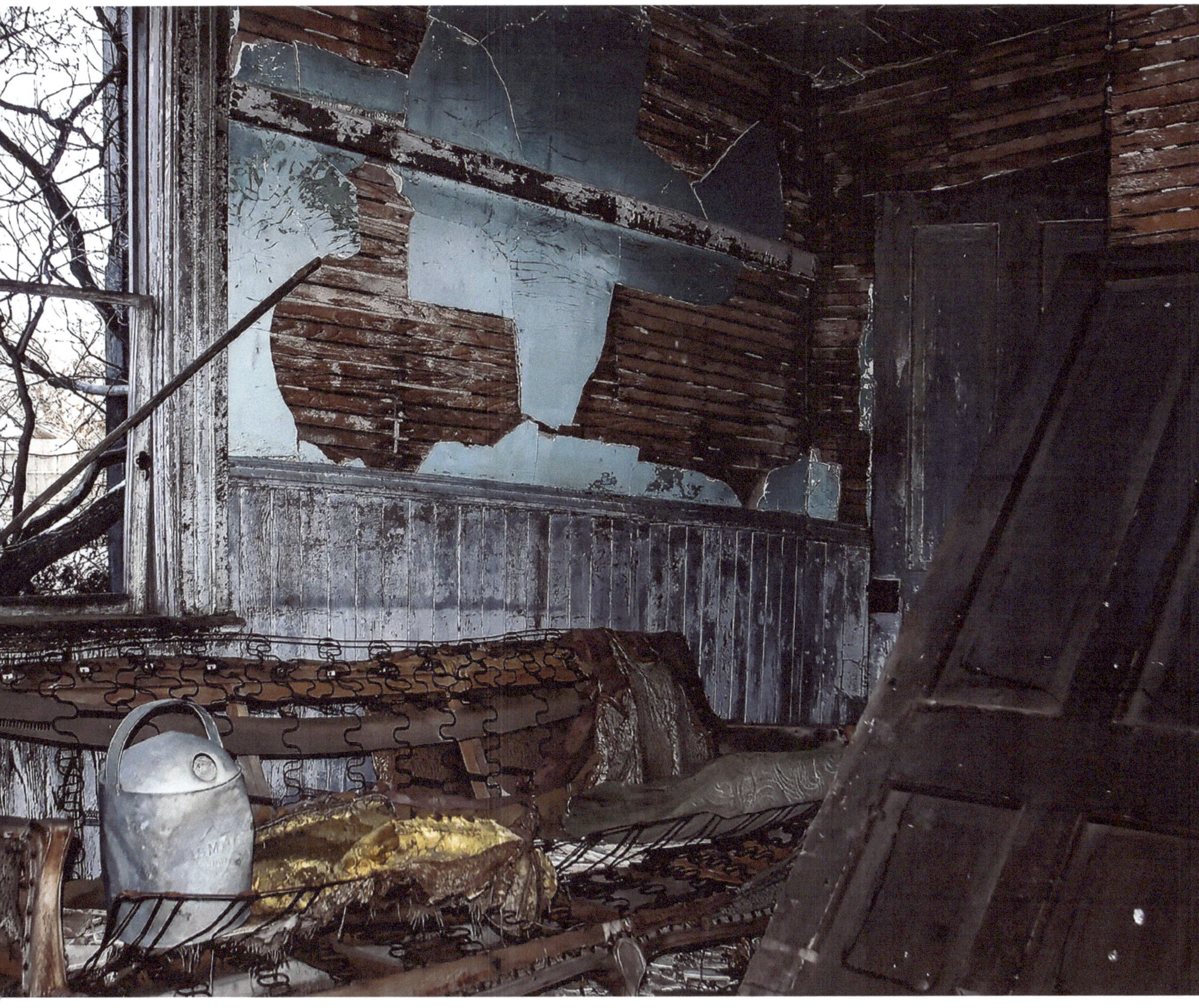

Rotting plaster, Saskatchewan (Cris Sia Moresca)

The lawn was claimed by brush and weeds
While inside rotting plaster fell.

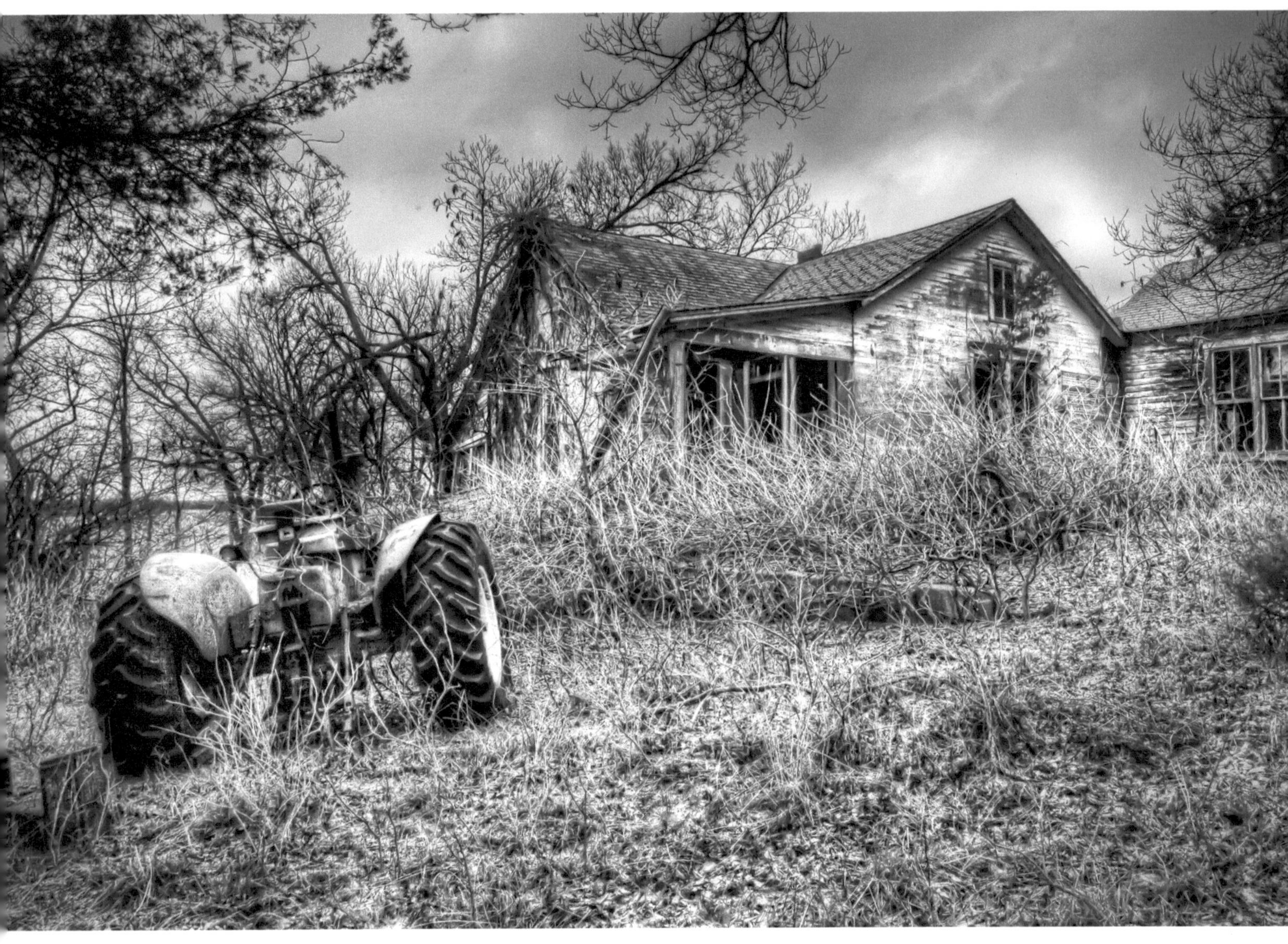

Ghost house and tractor, Cedar Point #2, Kansas (Dave McKane)

Whene'er I pass abandoned homes,
I sense a melancholy air

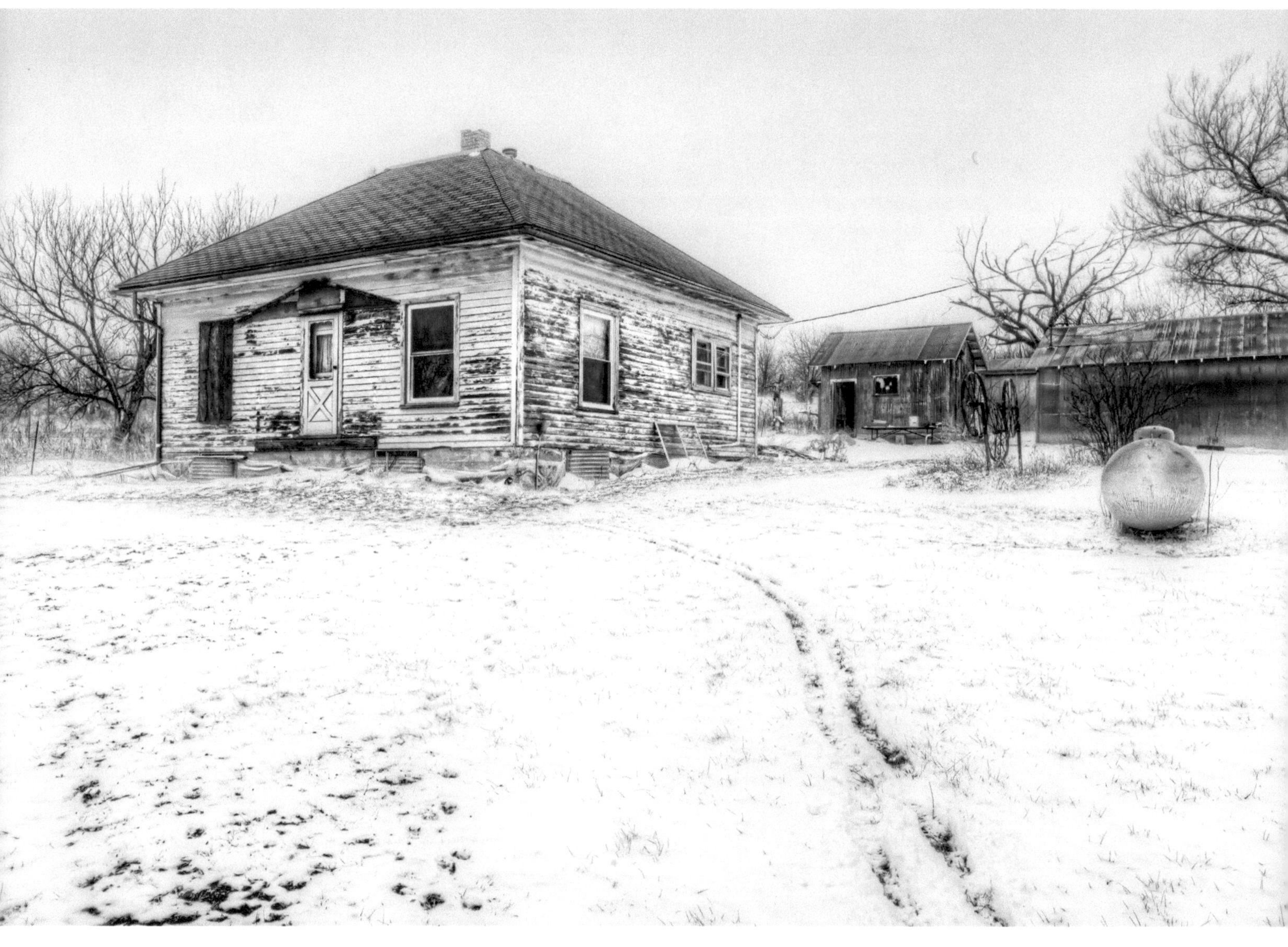

Ghost house, Overbrook #5, Kansas (Dave McKane)

'Bout things that were, or could have been,
The lives and values nurtured there.

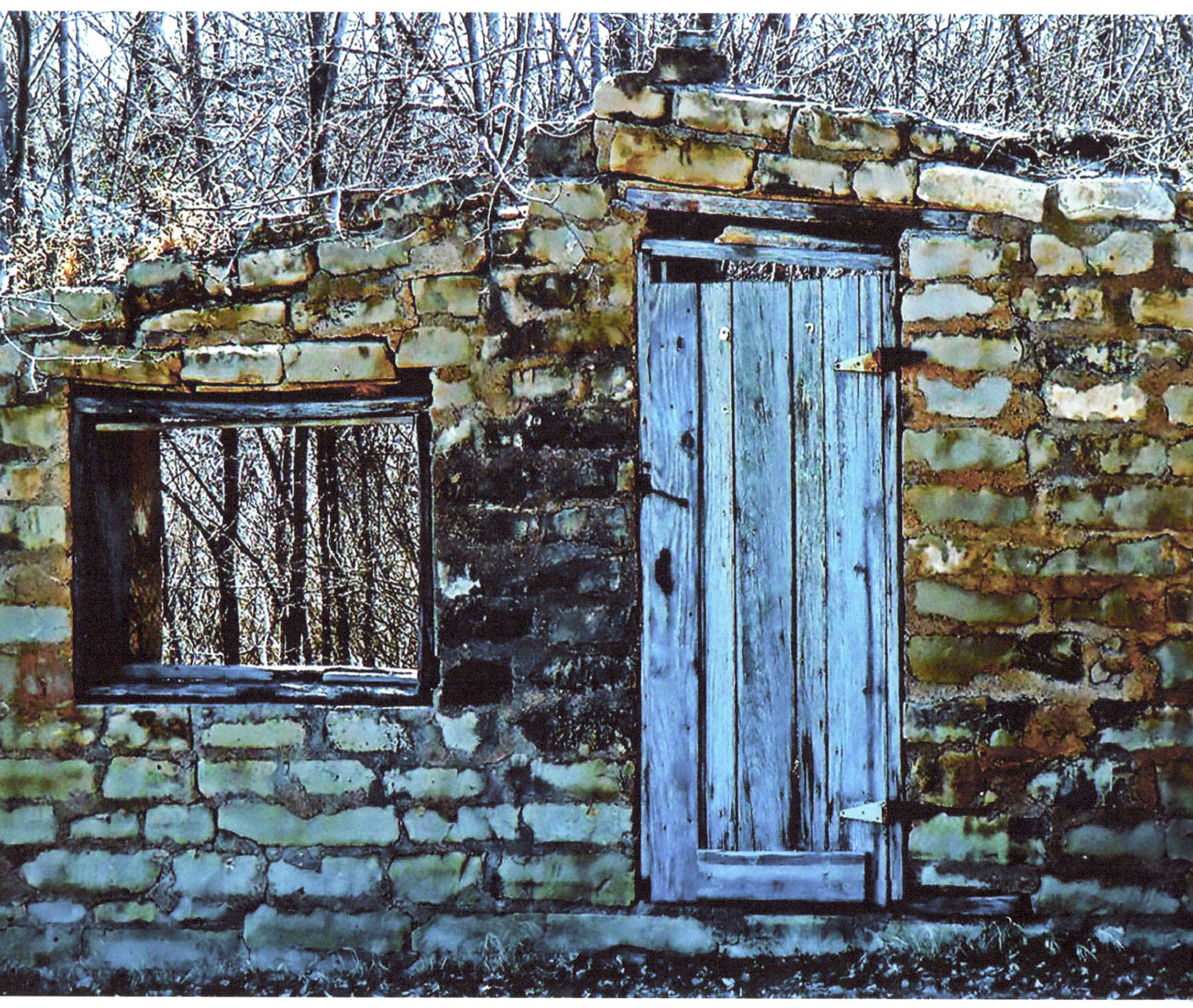

Stone wall, Kansas (Mark Pendergrass)

If walls could talk–but indeed they do,
Of love and laughter, pain and tears,

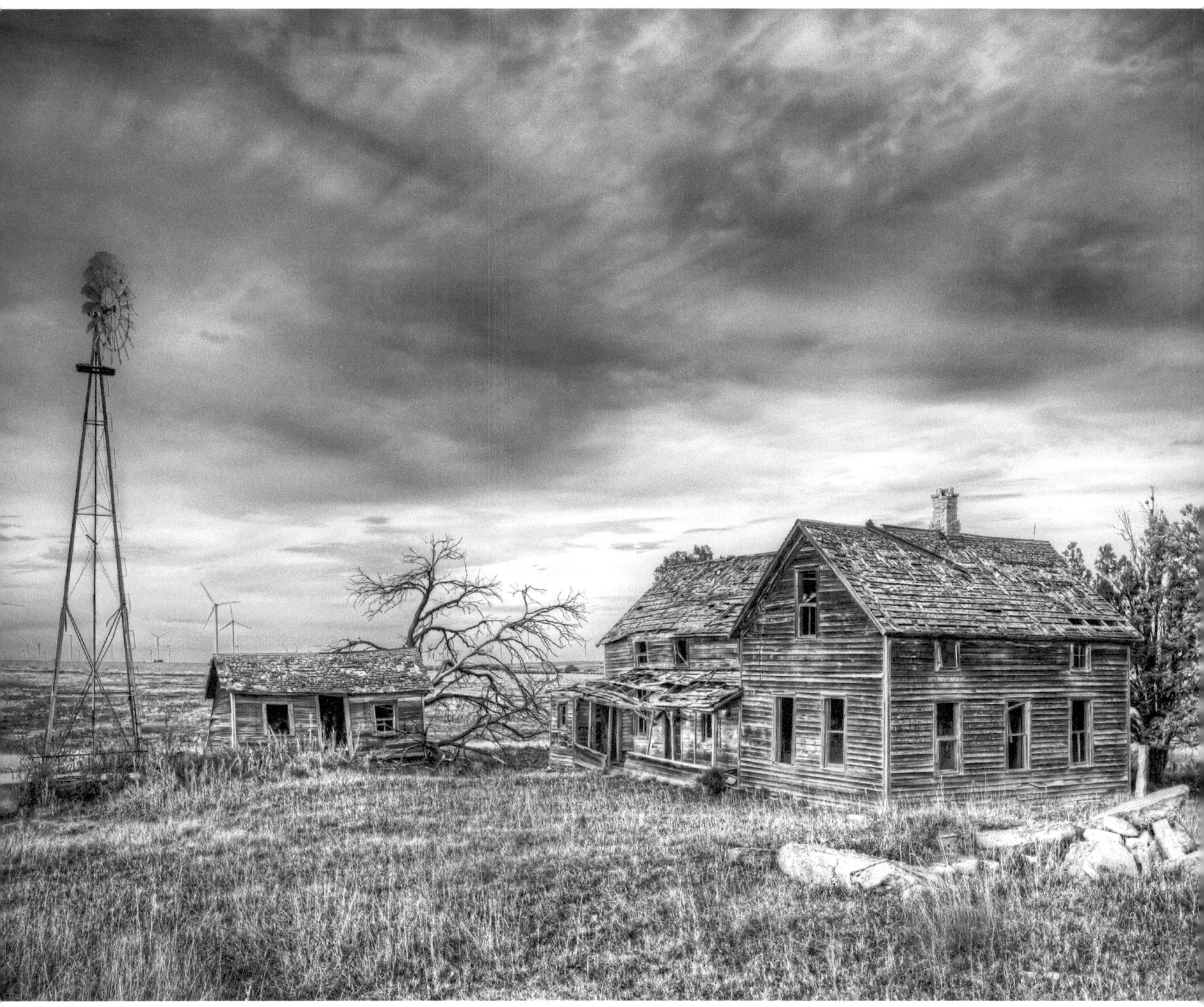

Ghost house, Ellsworth #2, Kansas (Dave McKane)

Of happy days and anxious hours,
Of passing years with hopes and fears.

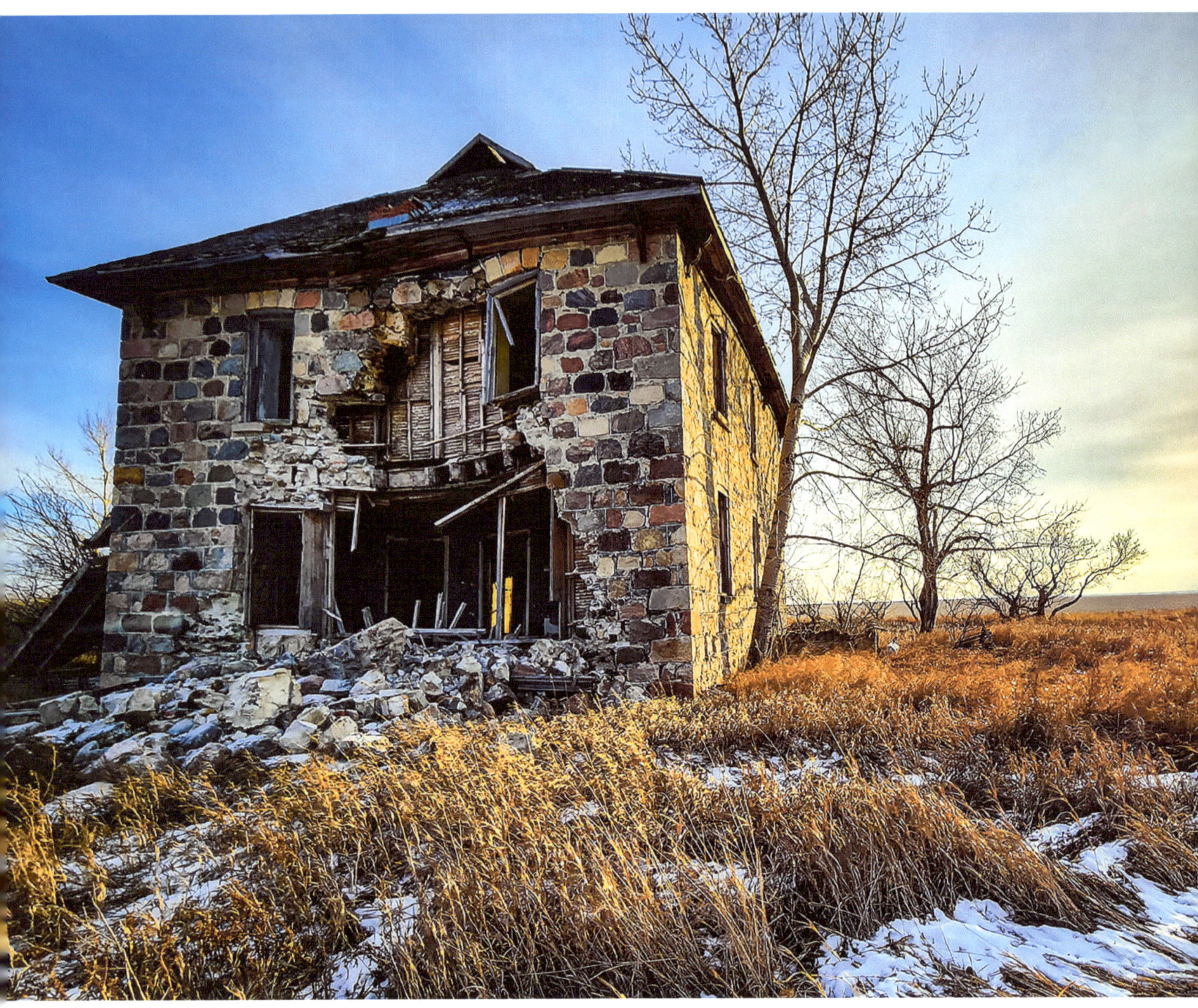

Amazing stonework, Saskatchewan (Cris Sia Moresca)

They only tattle what they've heard:
Of peace and strife, of pride or shame,

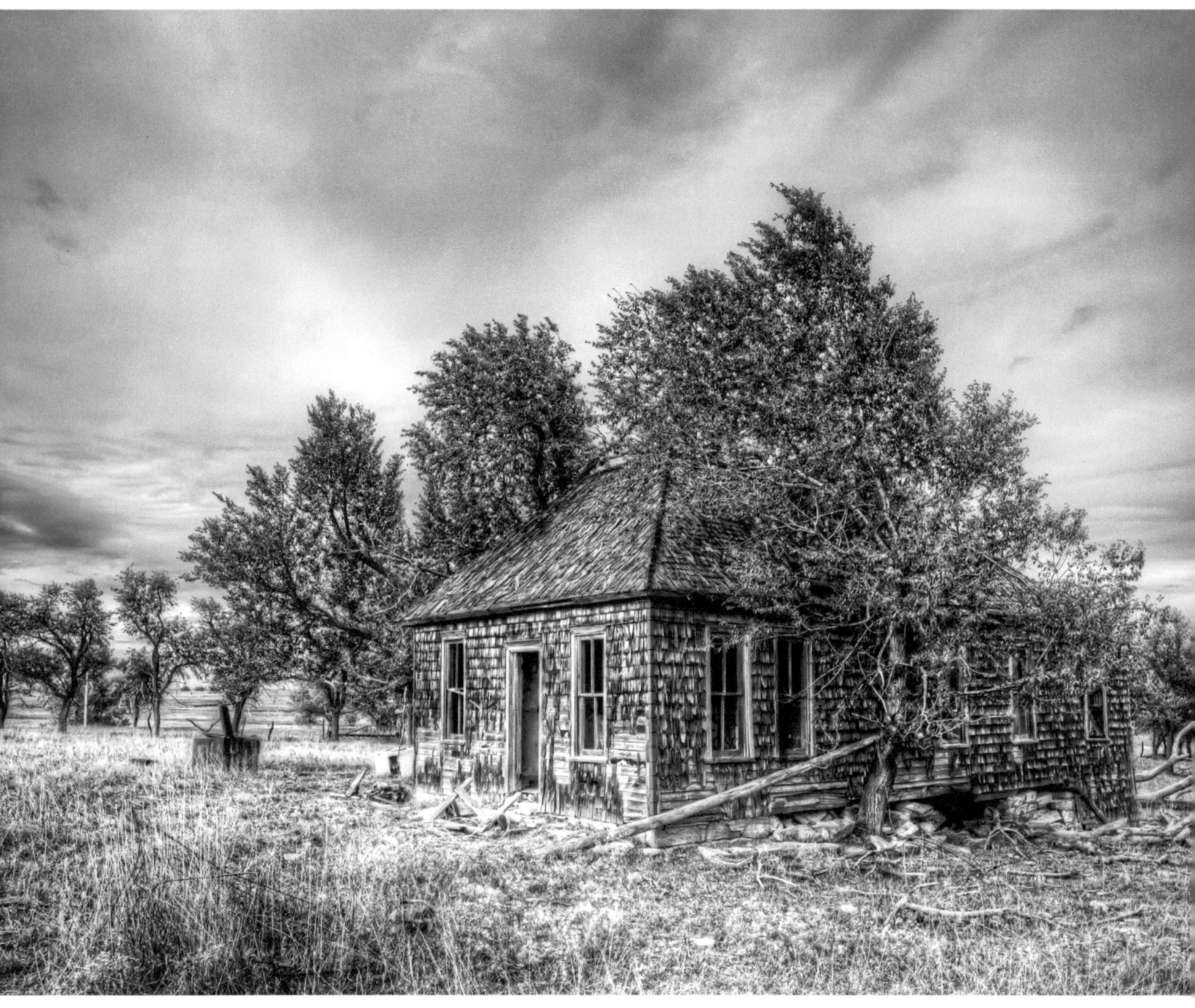

Ghost house, Ellsworth #3, Kansas (Dave McKane)

Of goodly words or those profane.

What might your house someday proclaim?

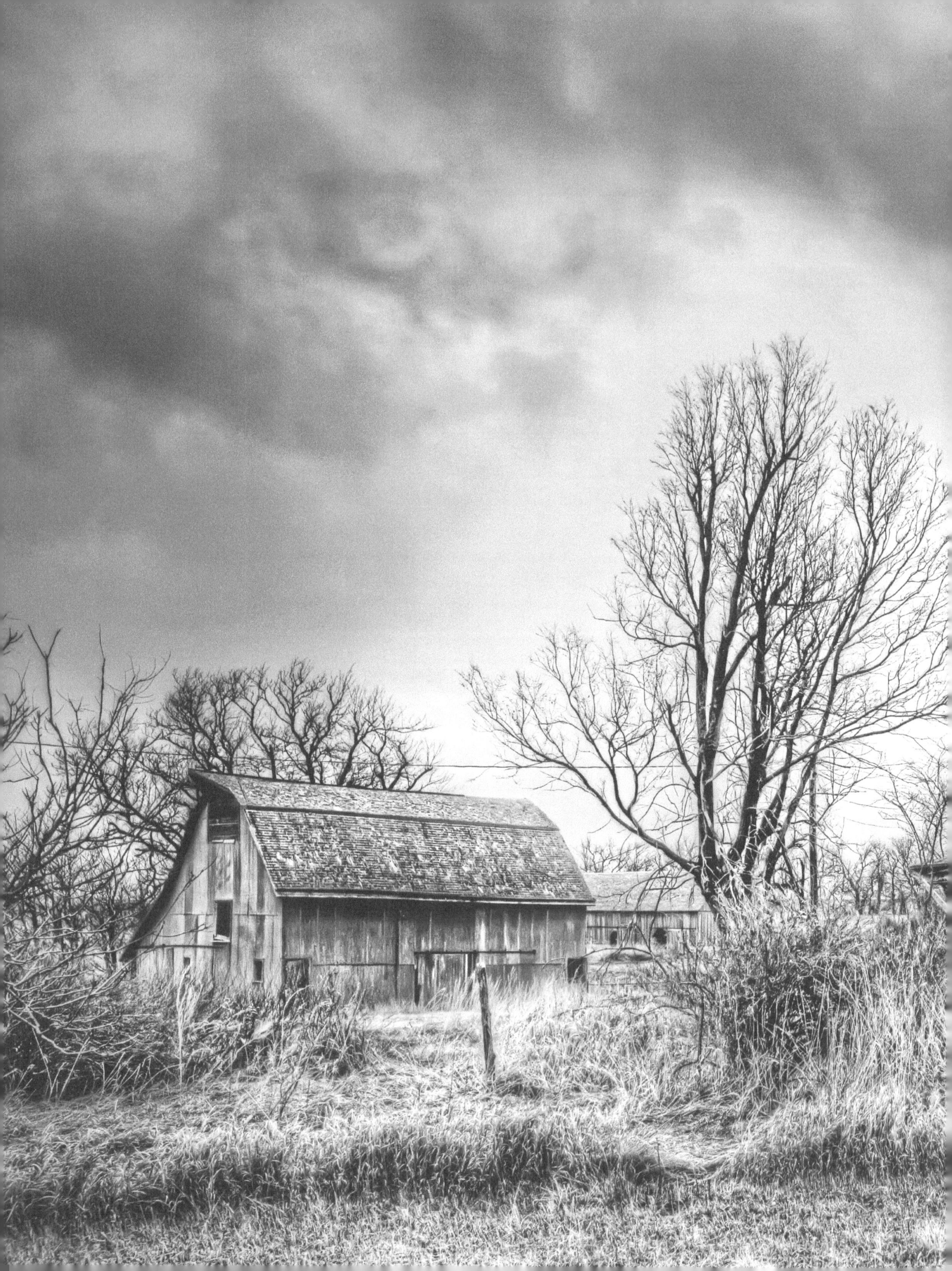

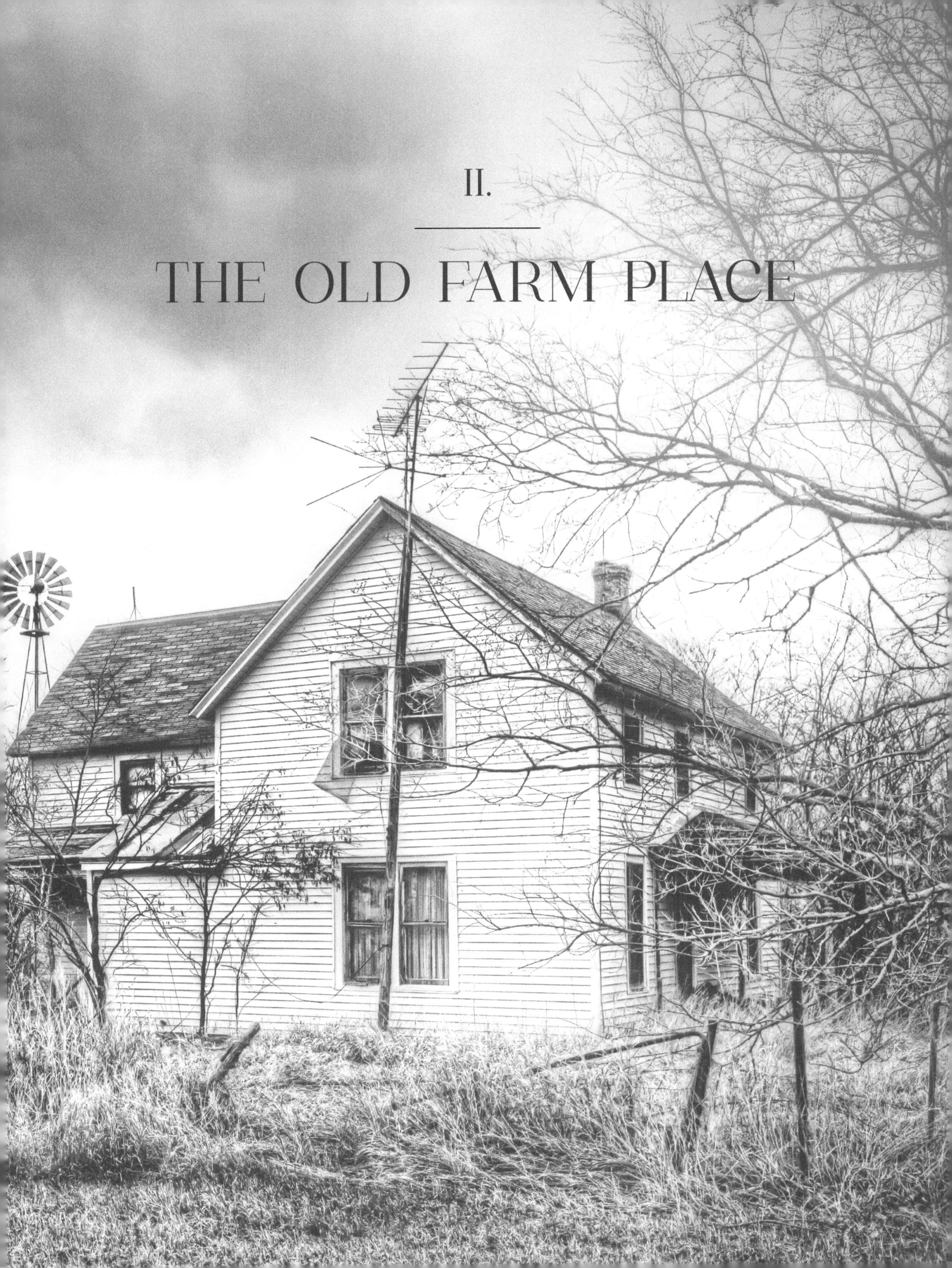

II.

THE OLD FARM PLACE

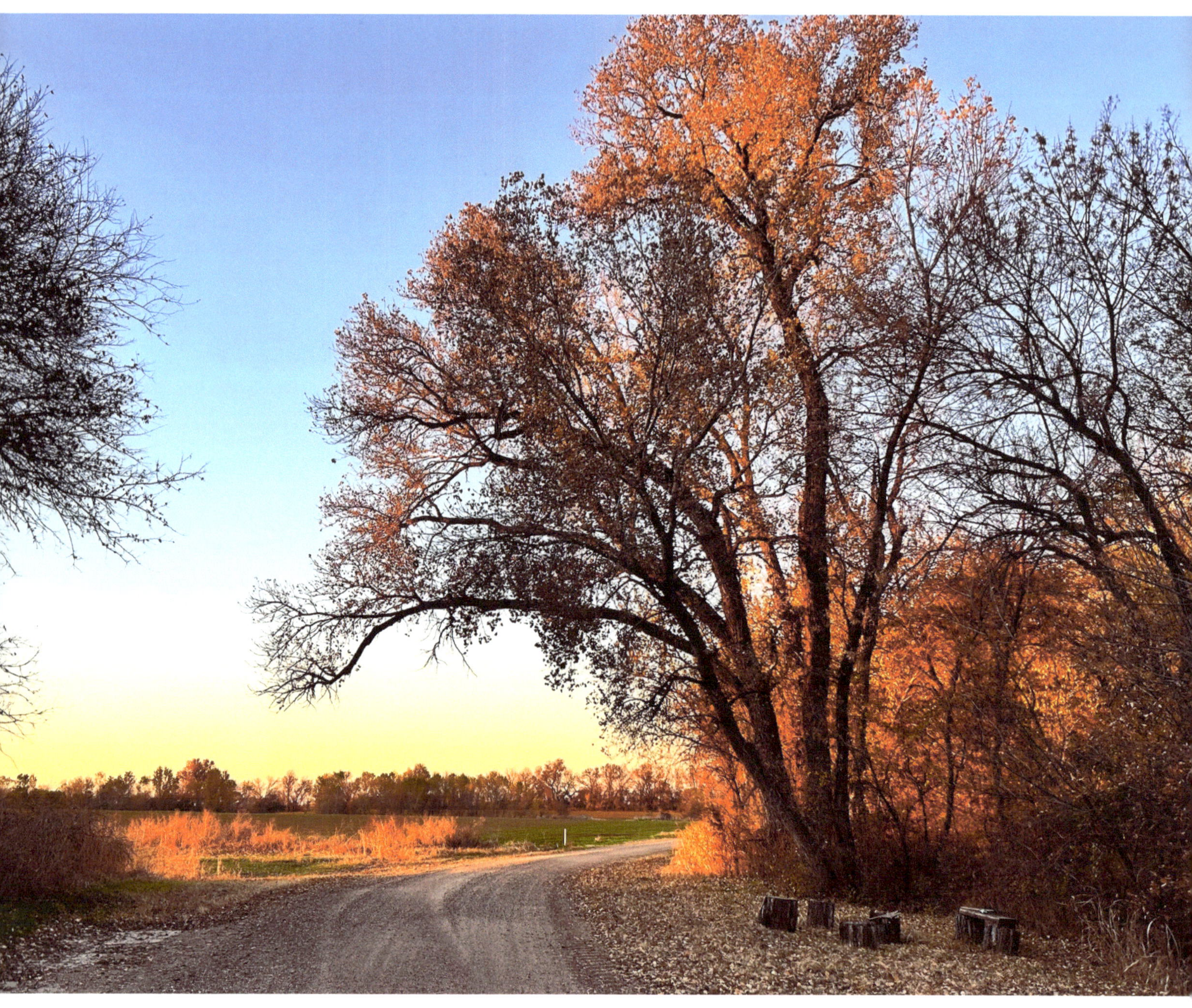

Gravelly lane, Kansas (Mark Pendergrass)

In the far Ozark hills there's a gravelly lane
And a place that stirs feelings too hard to contain.

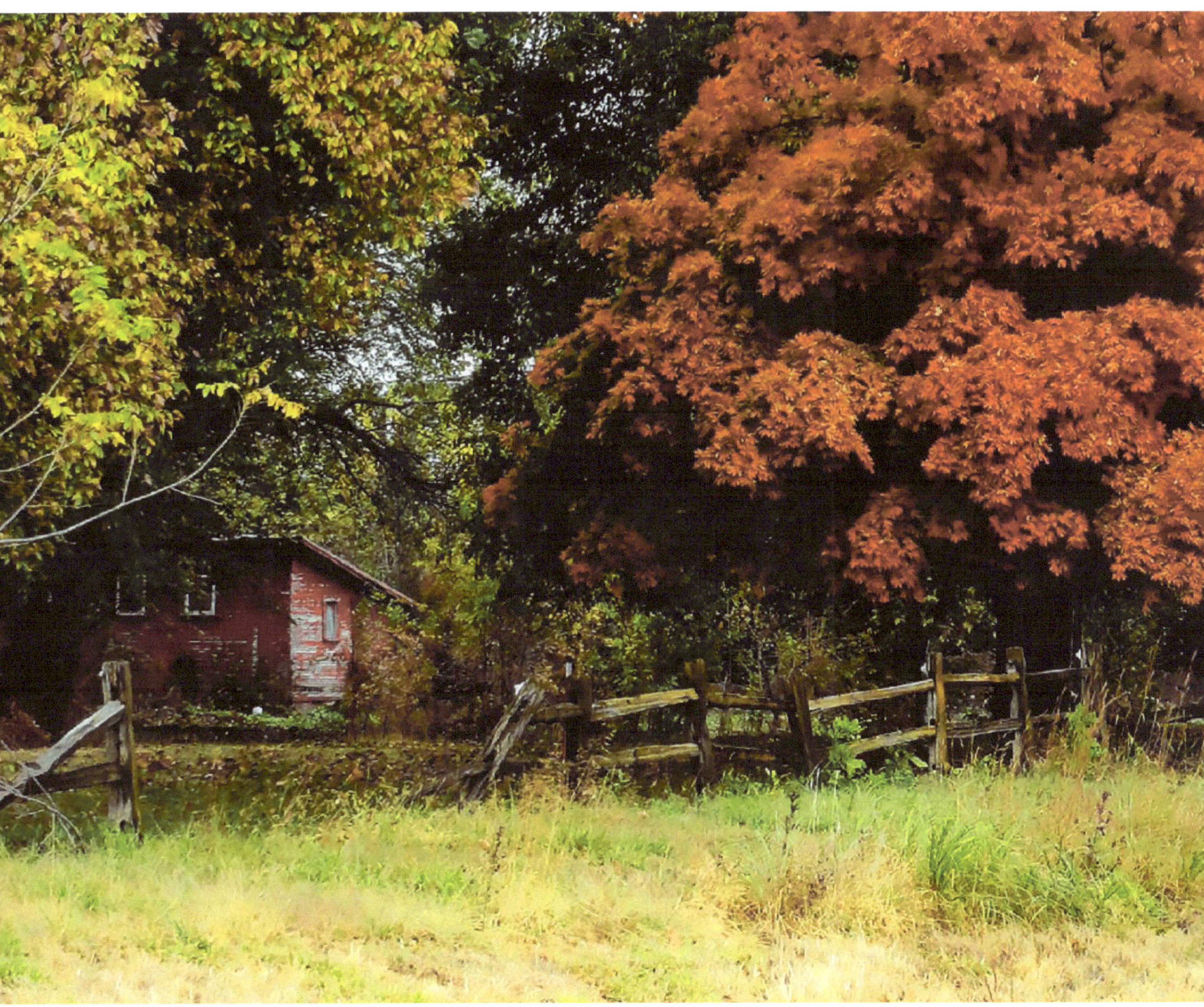

Autumn trees, Kansas (Mark Pendergrass)

Here the sweet lilacs bloomed and the hollyhocks too,
And there 'long the fence was where daffodils grew.

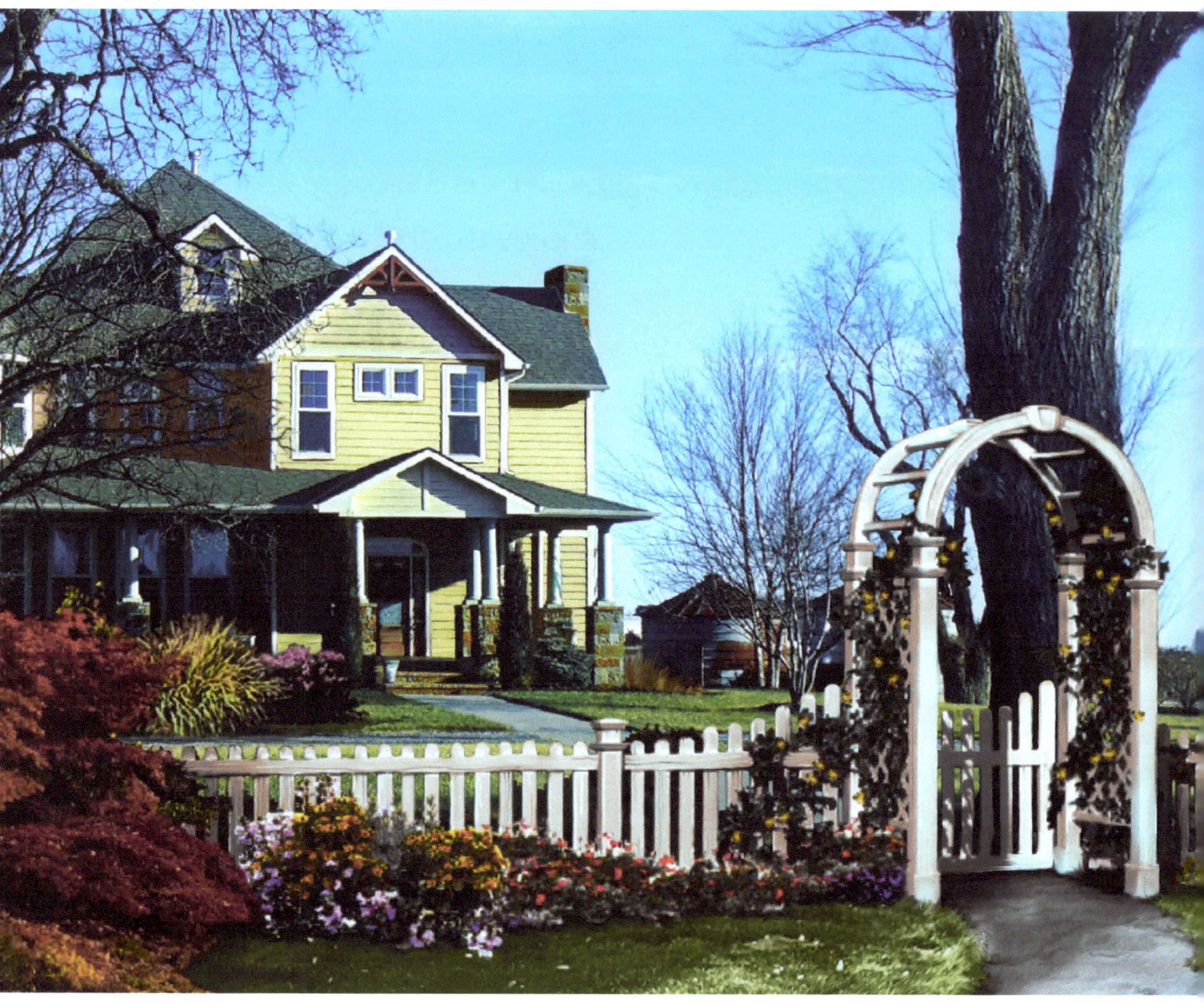

An inviting entryway, Kansas (Mark Pendergrass)

And the picture book yard all around the estate
Was approached through an arch with a small wooden gate.

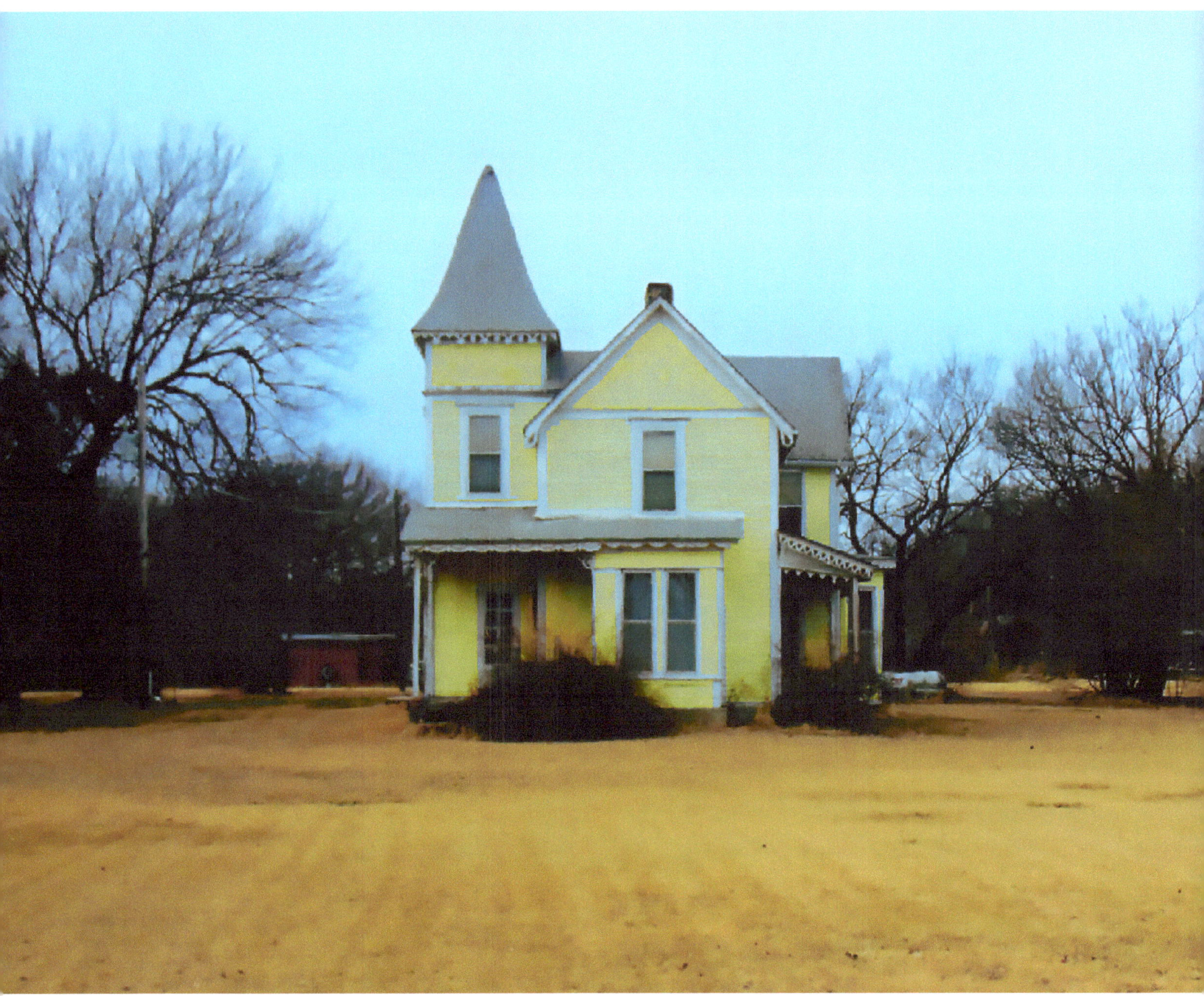

30 Yellow Victorian, Kansas (Mark Pendergrass)

Now the two-story house was bright yellow when new,
And it still was right homey, though faded in hue.

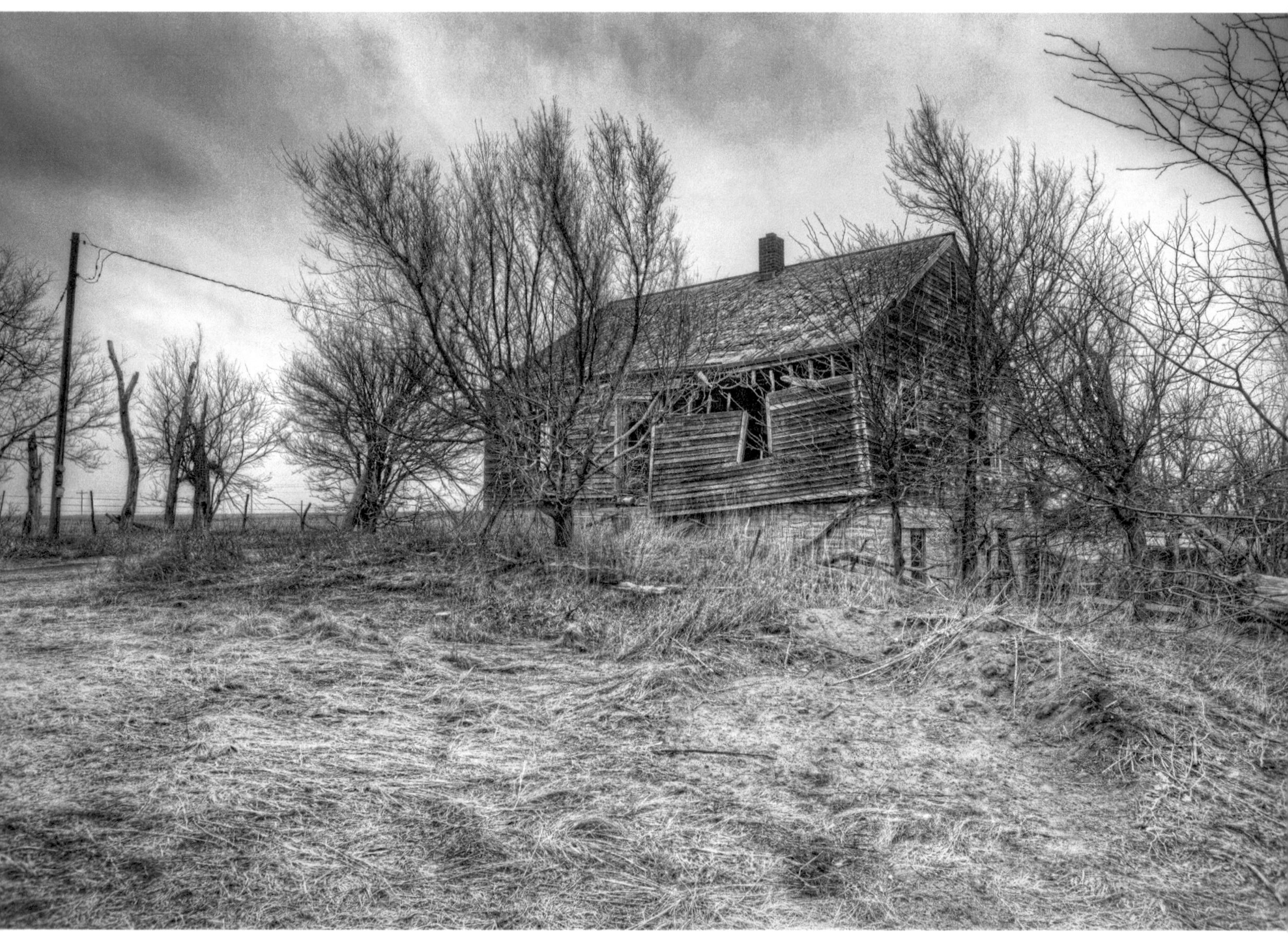

Ghost house, Ellsworth #5, Kansas (Dave McKane)

Yet it stood quite erect on the brow of a hill
To provide a warm shelter 'gainst winter's deep chill,

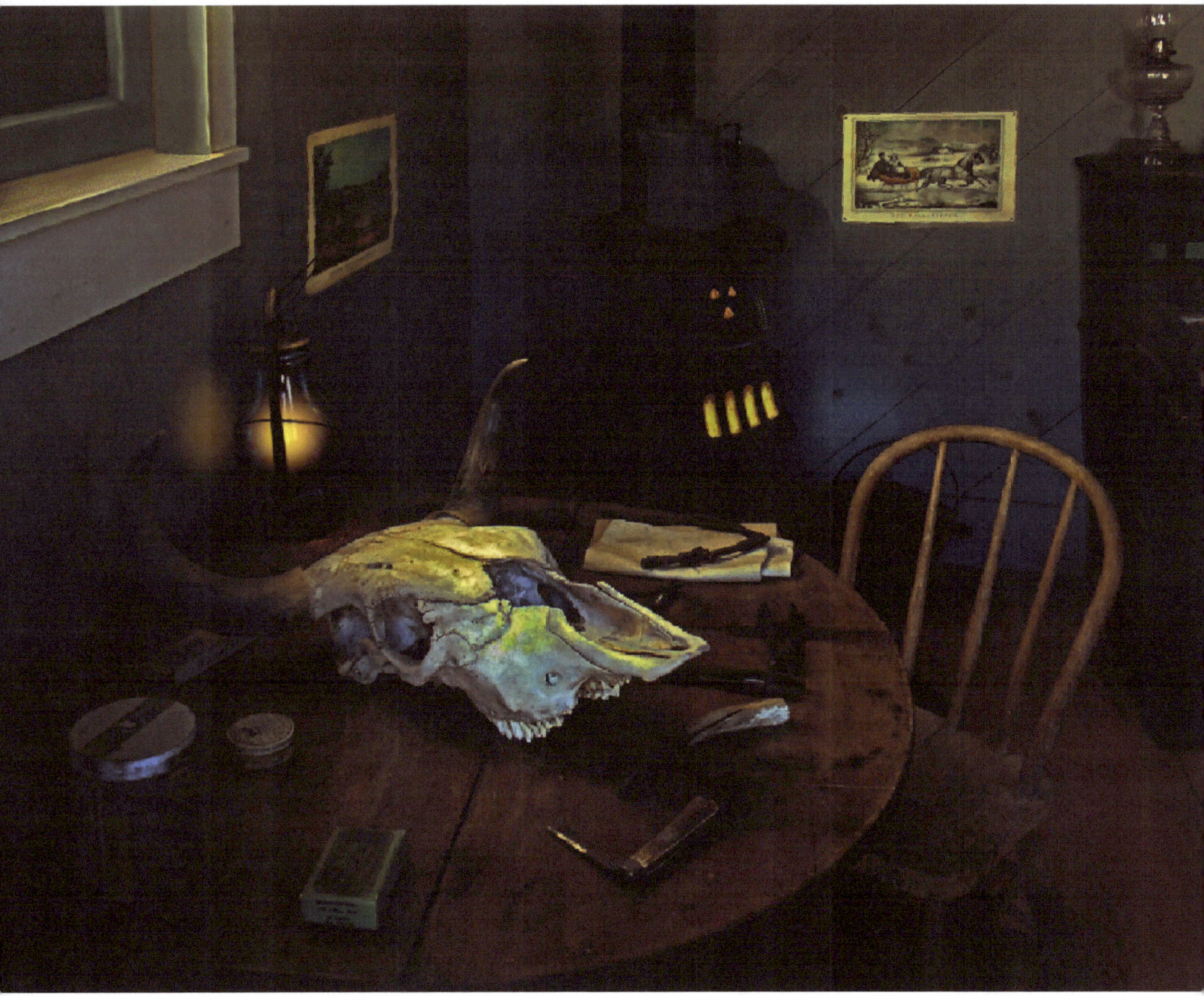

Rustic interior, Kansas (Mark Pendergrass)

When the kerosene lamps helped to hold back the night,
While the wood-burning stove lent its flickering light.

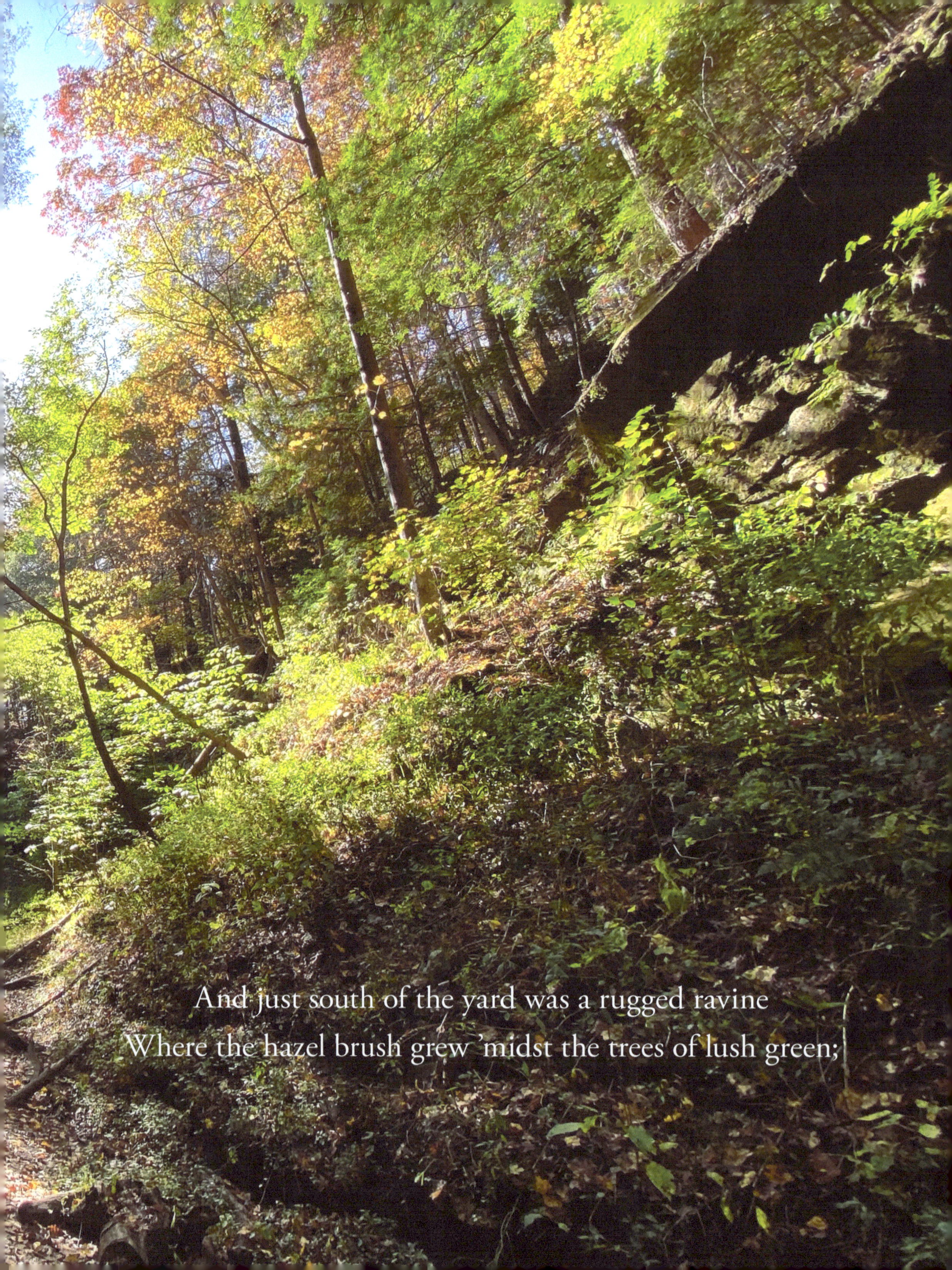

And just south of the yard was a rugged ravine
Where the hazel brush grew 'midst the trees of lush green;

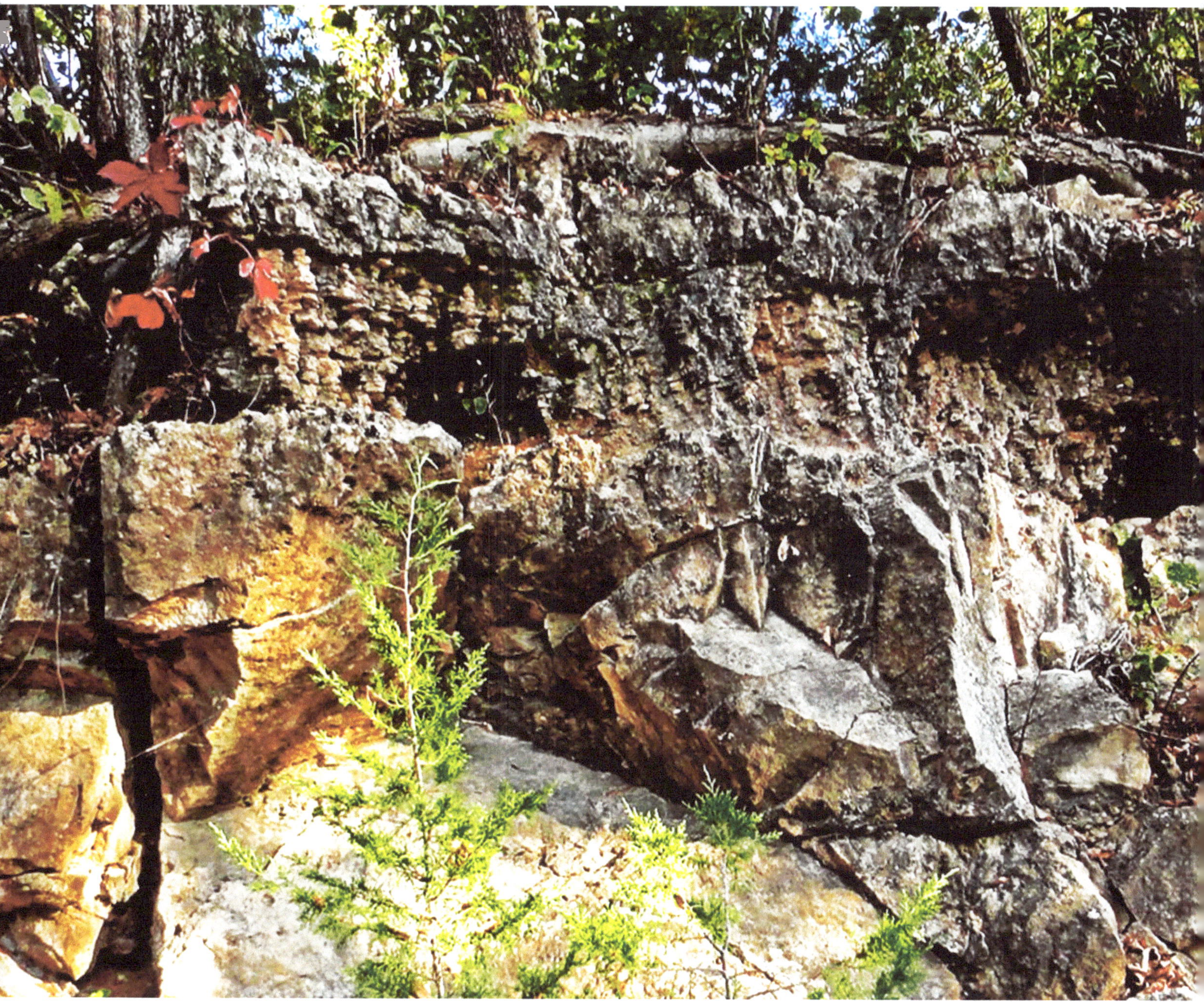

Left: Ravine (Mark Murphy)   Rocky spring, Kansas (Mark Pendergrass)

For a spring surfaced there 'neath a dank ledge of rock,
And it furnished refreshment for man and his stock.

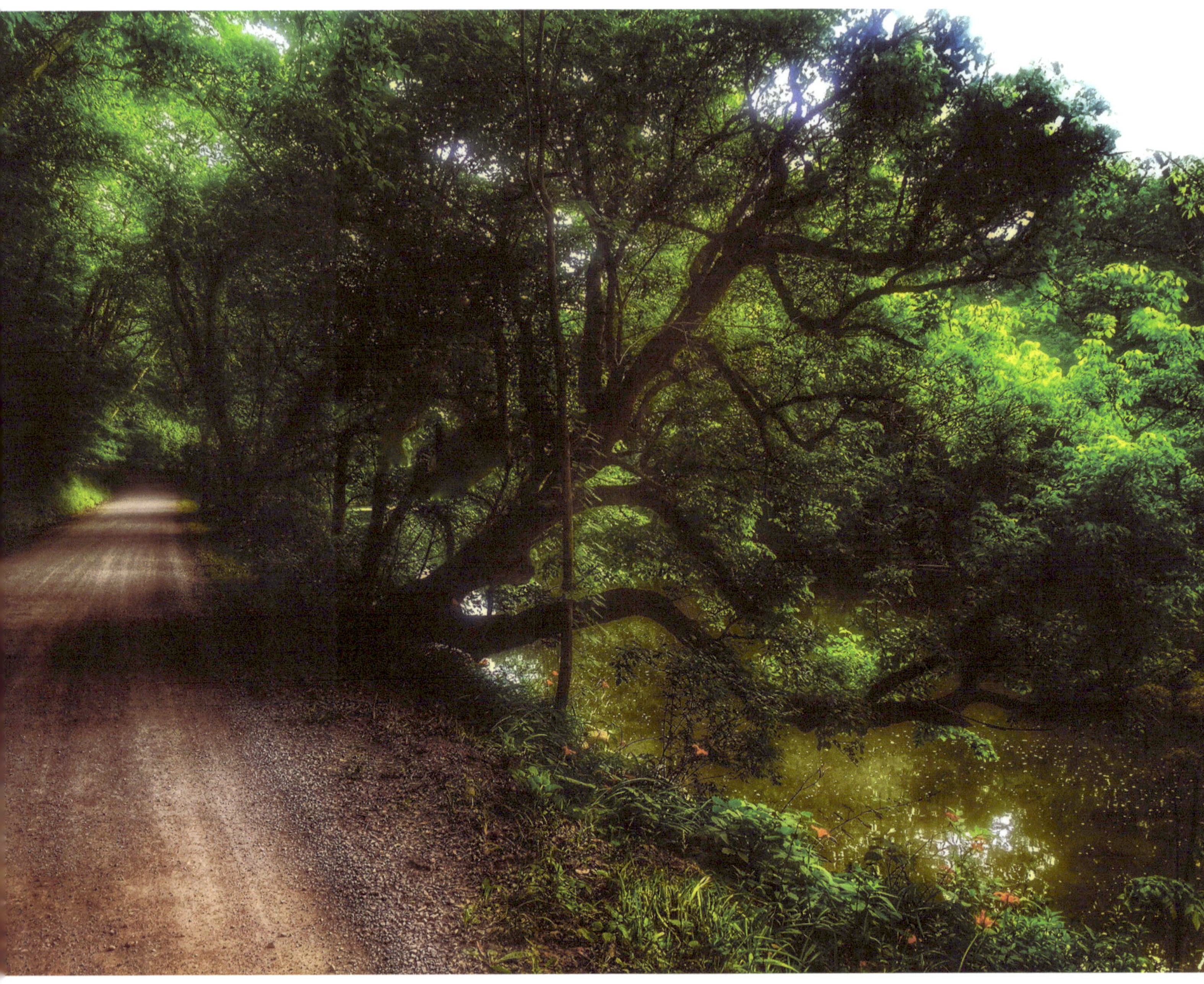

Dirt road and slow creek (Mark Murphy)

In the summers of drought and the months when it snowed,
And abundant supply of the cool water flowed.

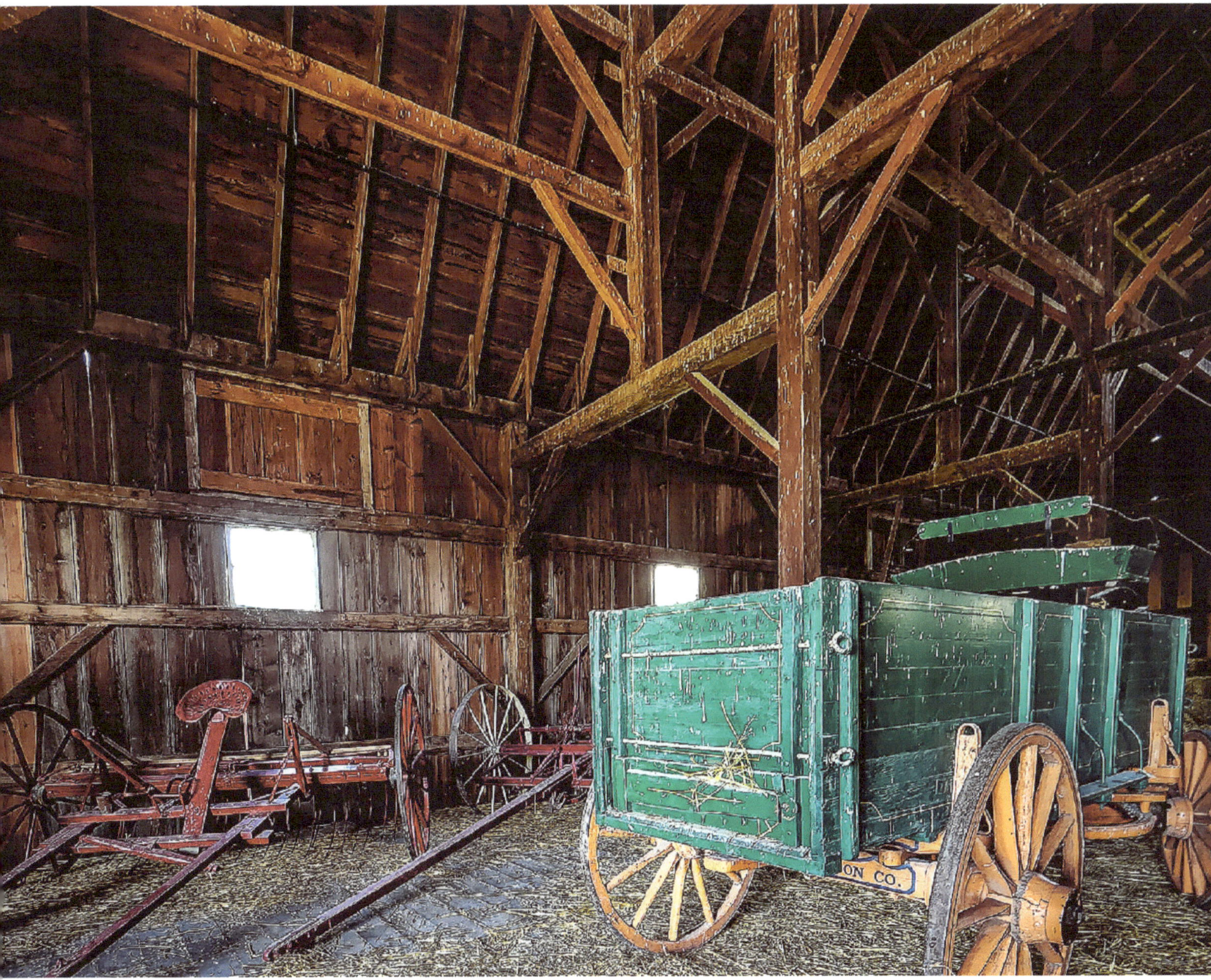

Barn interior, Saskatchewan (Cris Sia Moresca)

There the barn was full-framed, with its future assured.

Massive timbers, with mortise and tenon secured,

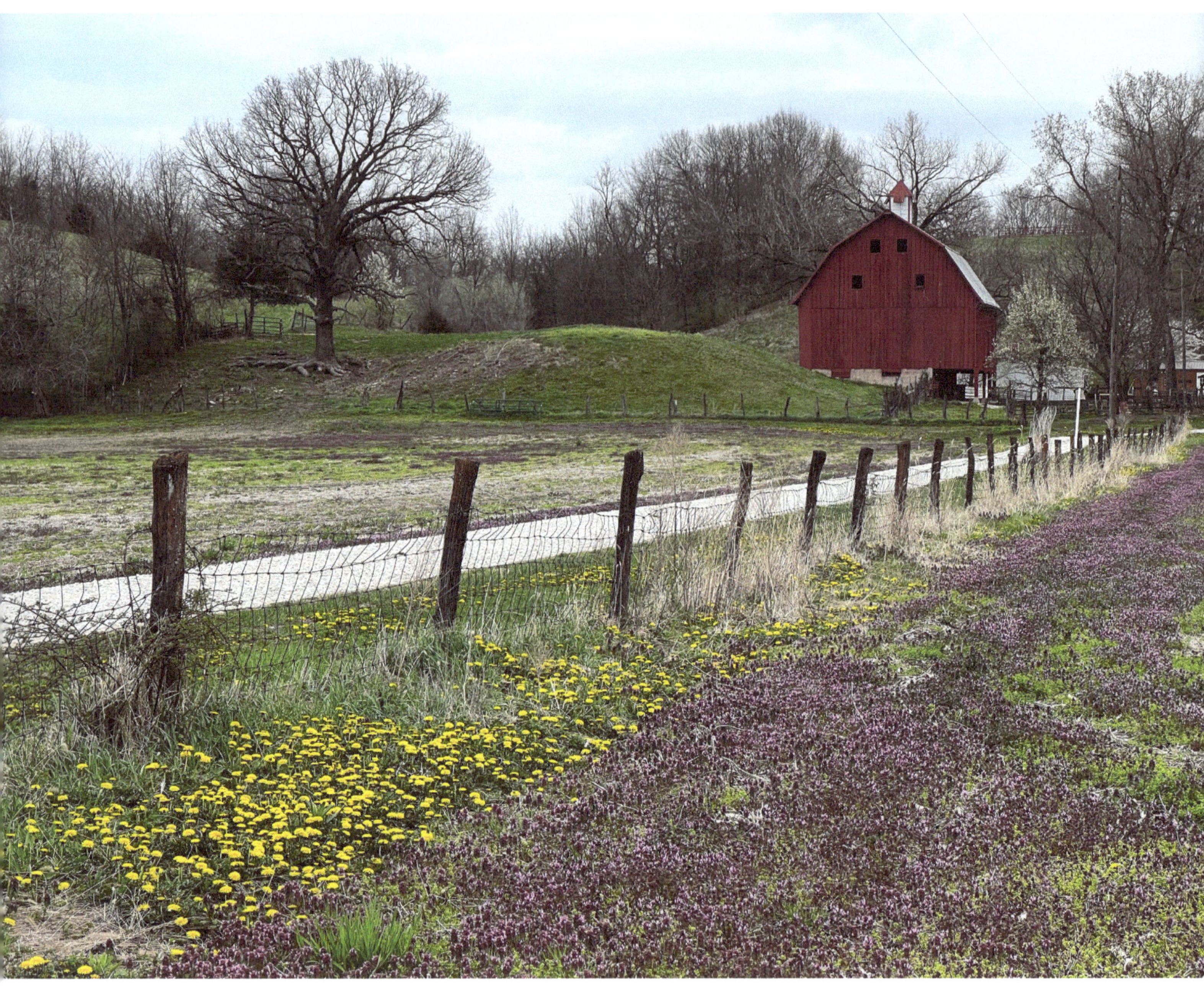

Barn on hill (Mark Murphy)

Held the huge structure true in the side of the steep
That commanded a view of the valley's broad sweep.

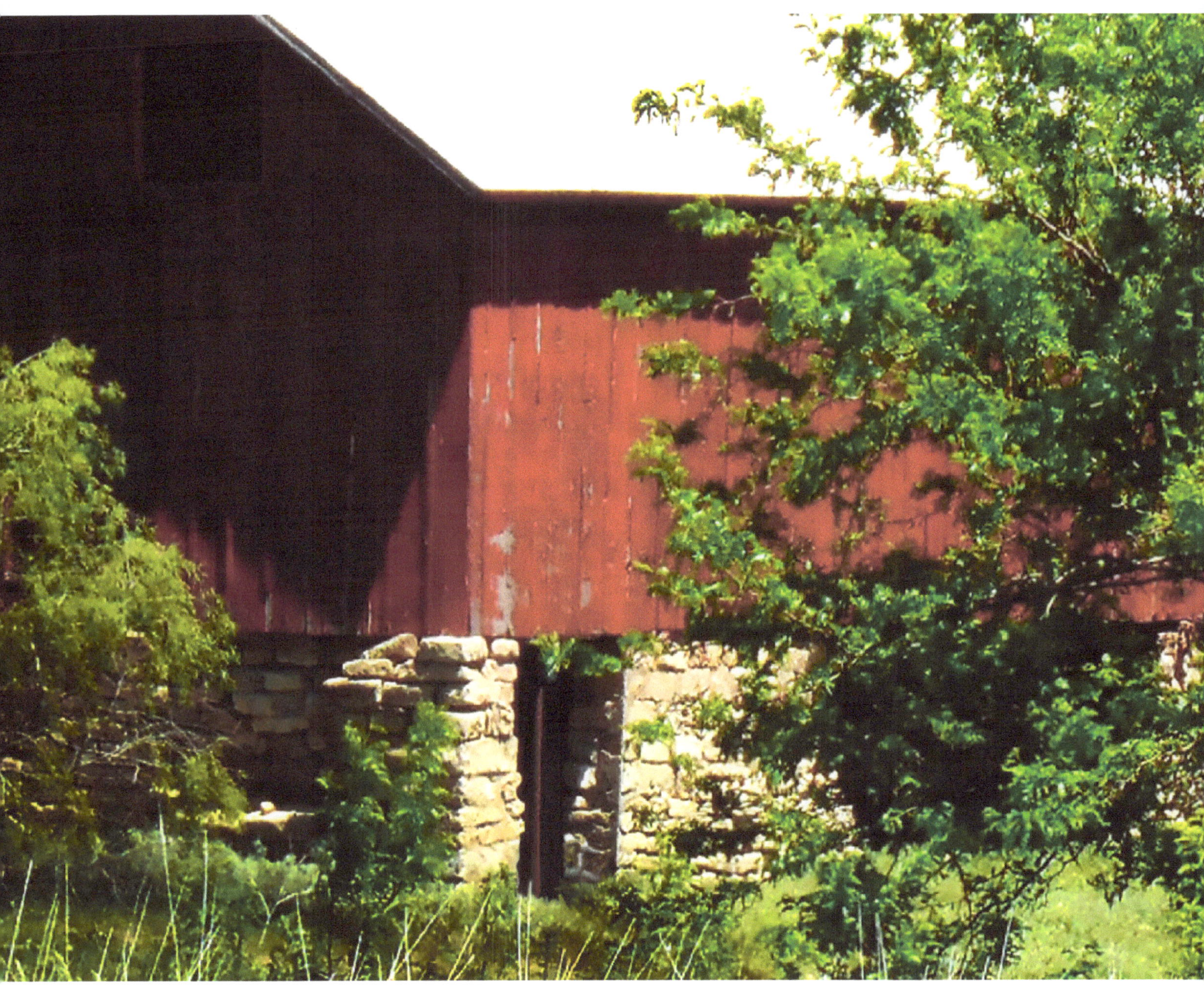

Red barn, Kansas (Mark Pendergrass)

And the oak trees grew thick on the boulder-strewn hill
Near the house and the barn, which were built with such skill.

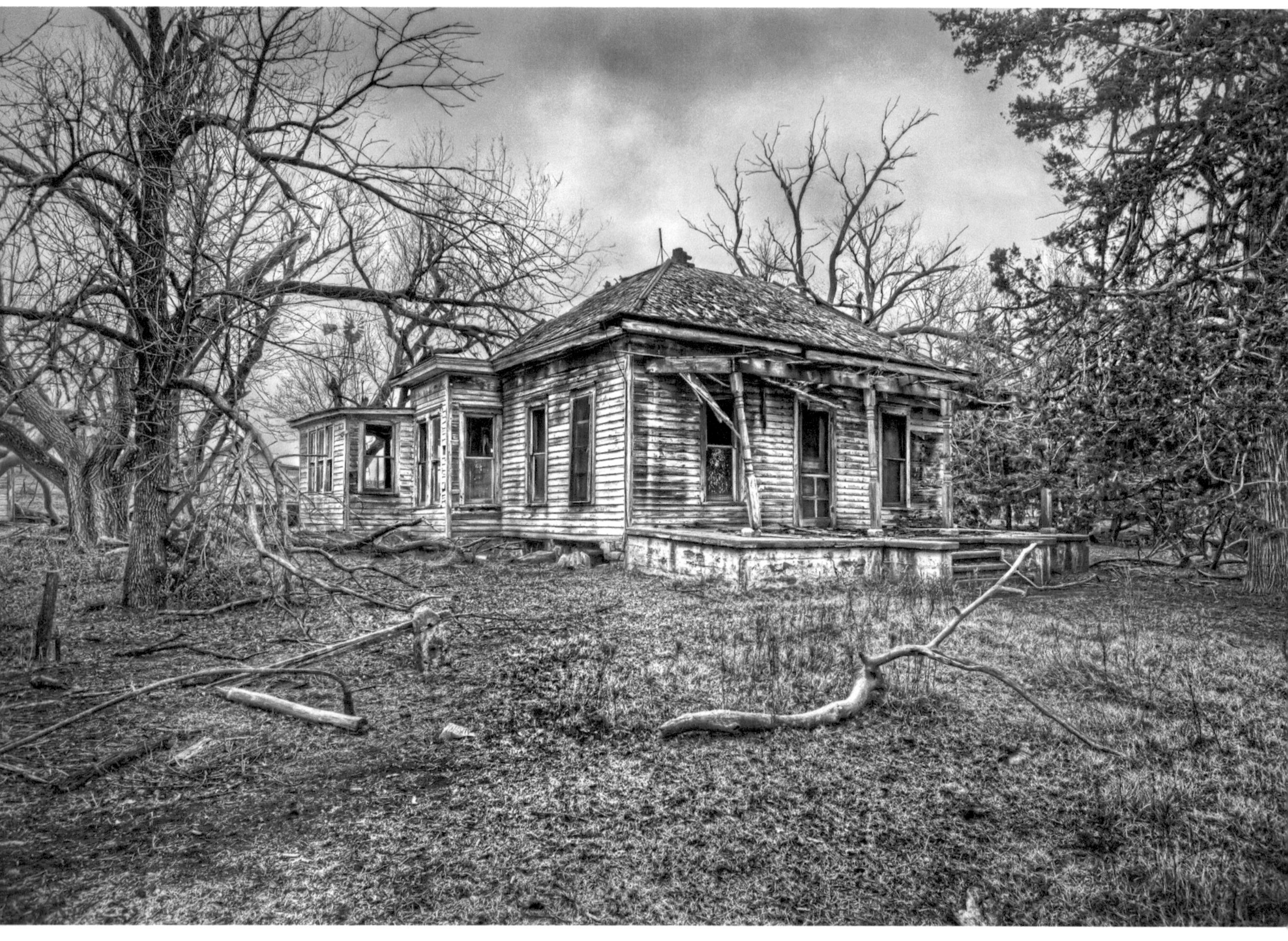

Ghost house, Ellsworth #6, Kansas (Dave McKane)

Now the desolate house, gaunt and gray, barely stands
As a shelter for rodents and birds of all kinds;

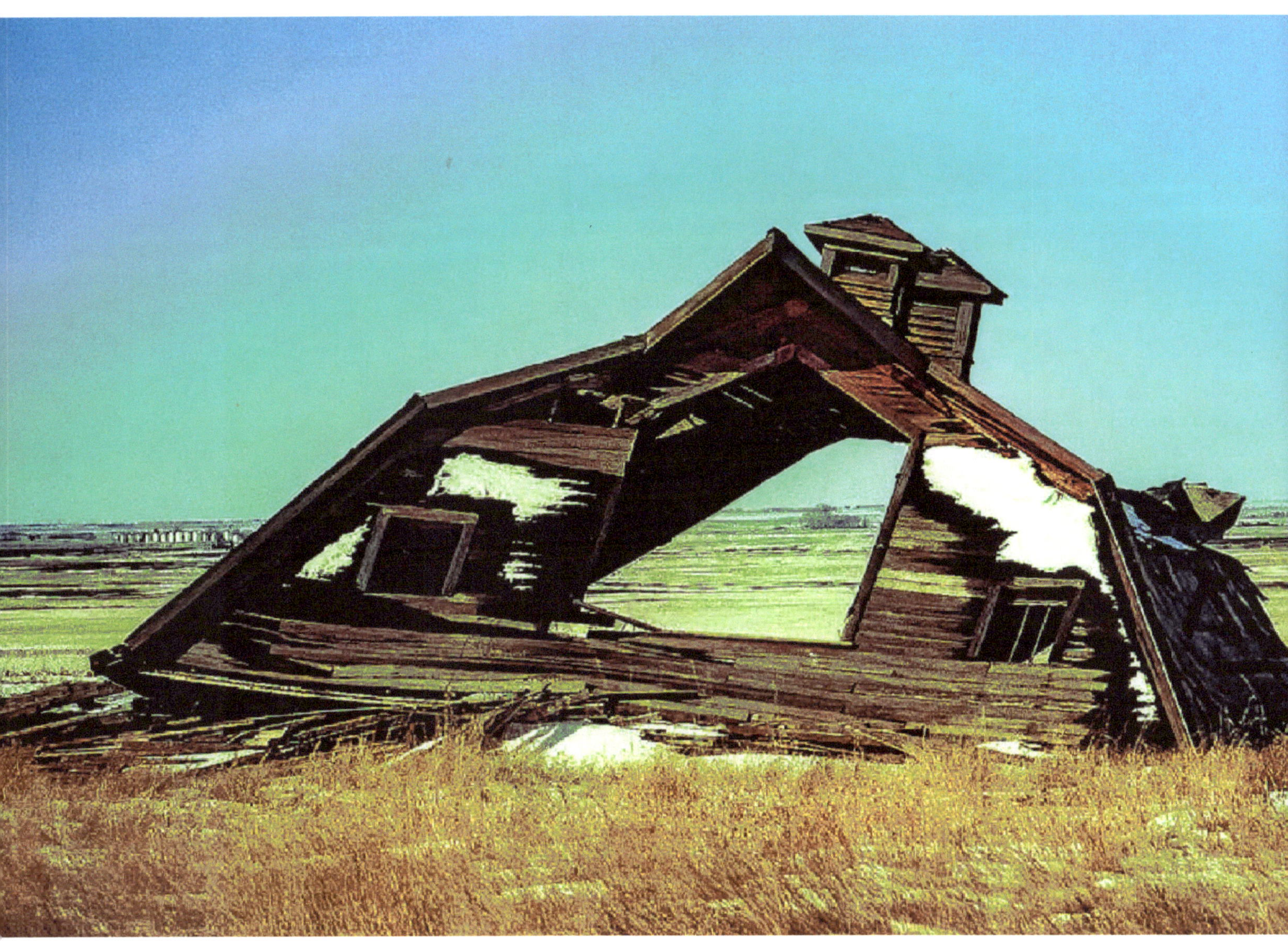

Collapsed barn, Saskatchewan (Cris Sia Moresca)

And the barn has collapsed to the basement's dirt floor,
While the spring house is gone, and the fence is no more.

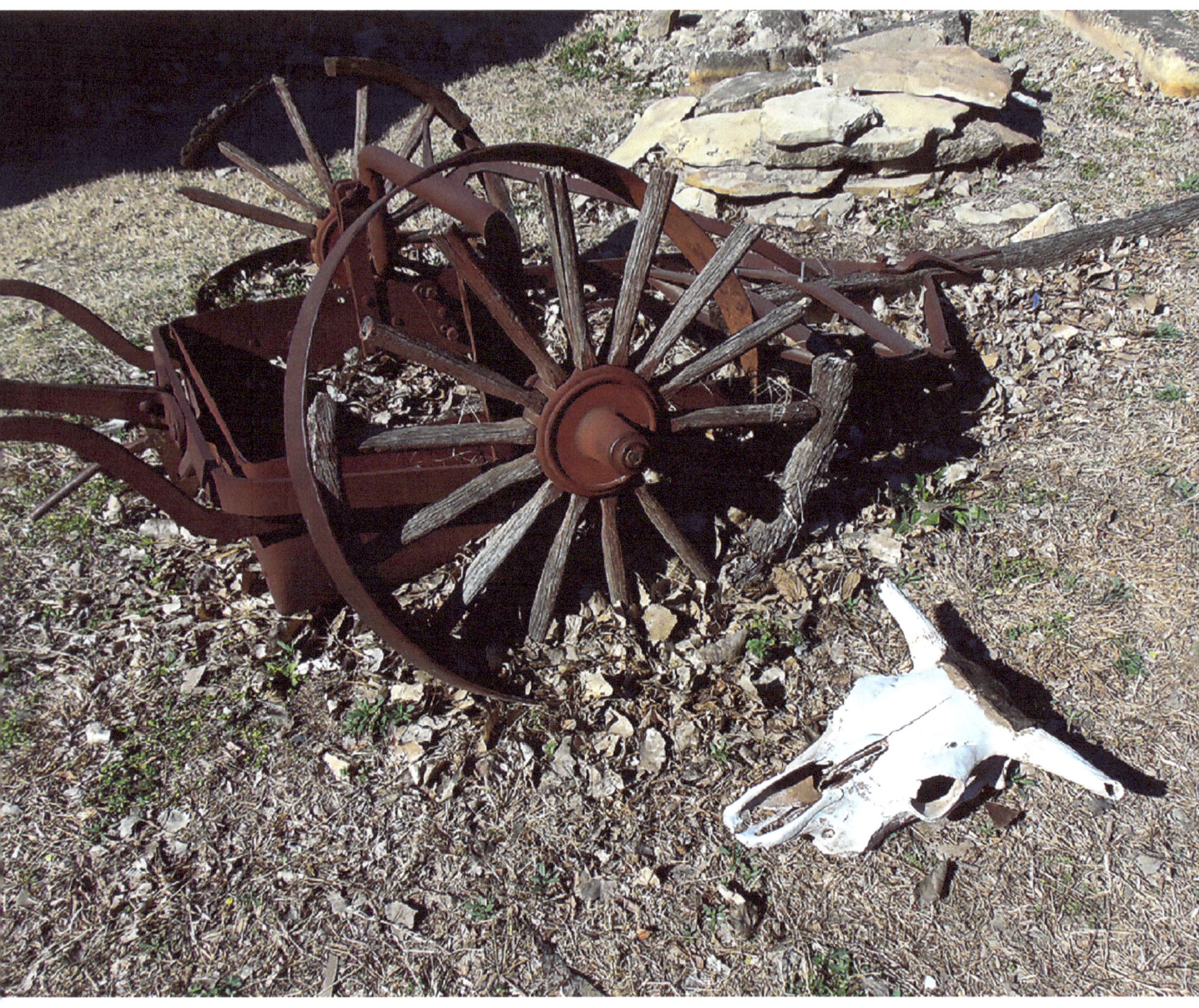

Cart and skull, Kansas (Mark Pendergrass)

Like the folks who once dwelt there, they've lived their life spans,
And the wild things run free through these haunts which were man's.

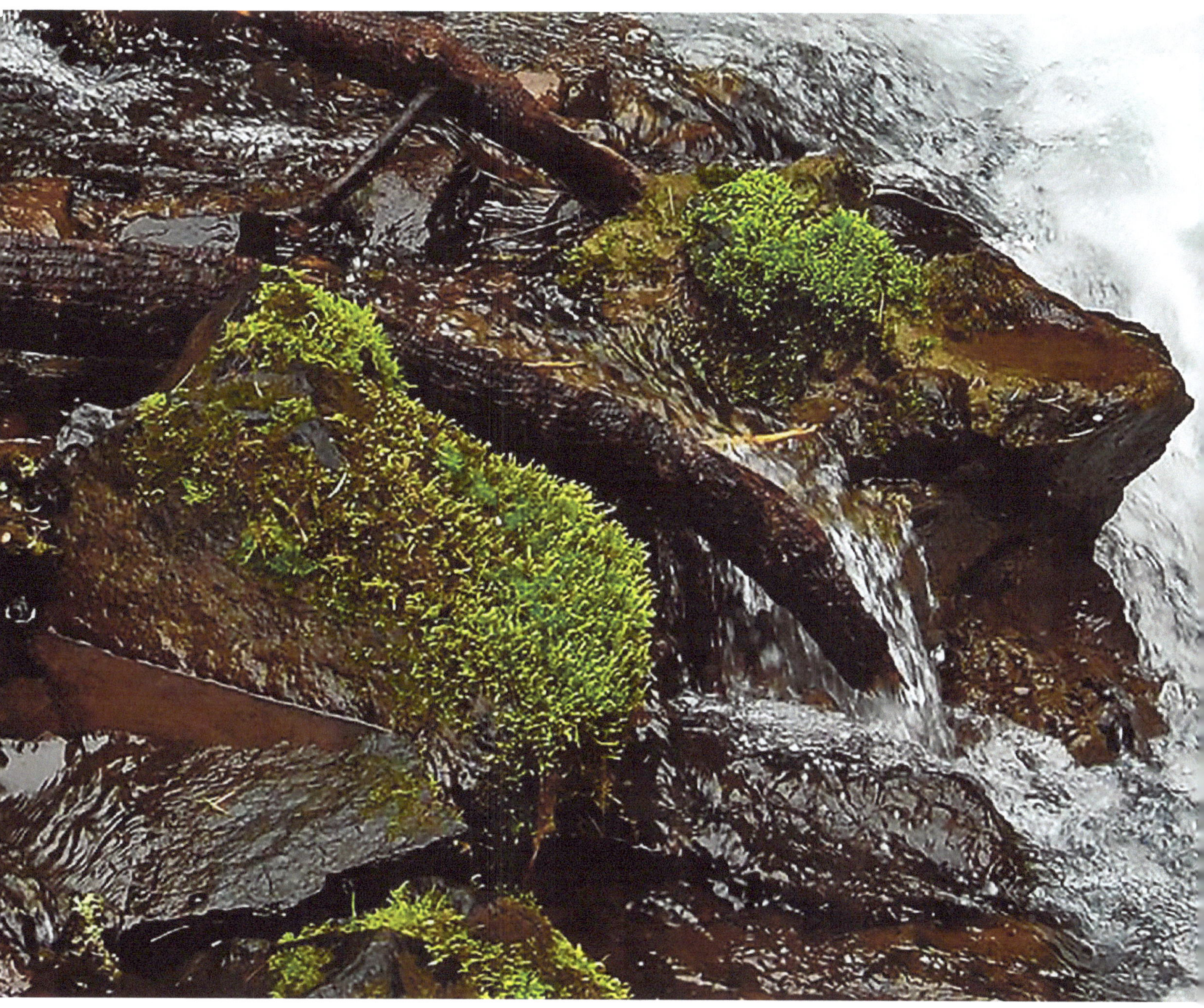

Rocky stream (Mark Murphy)

But the spring flows on still down its rocky defile;
And the oaks, more profusely than ever, meanwhile

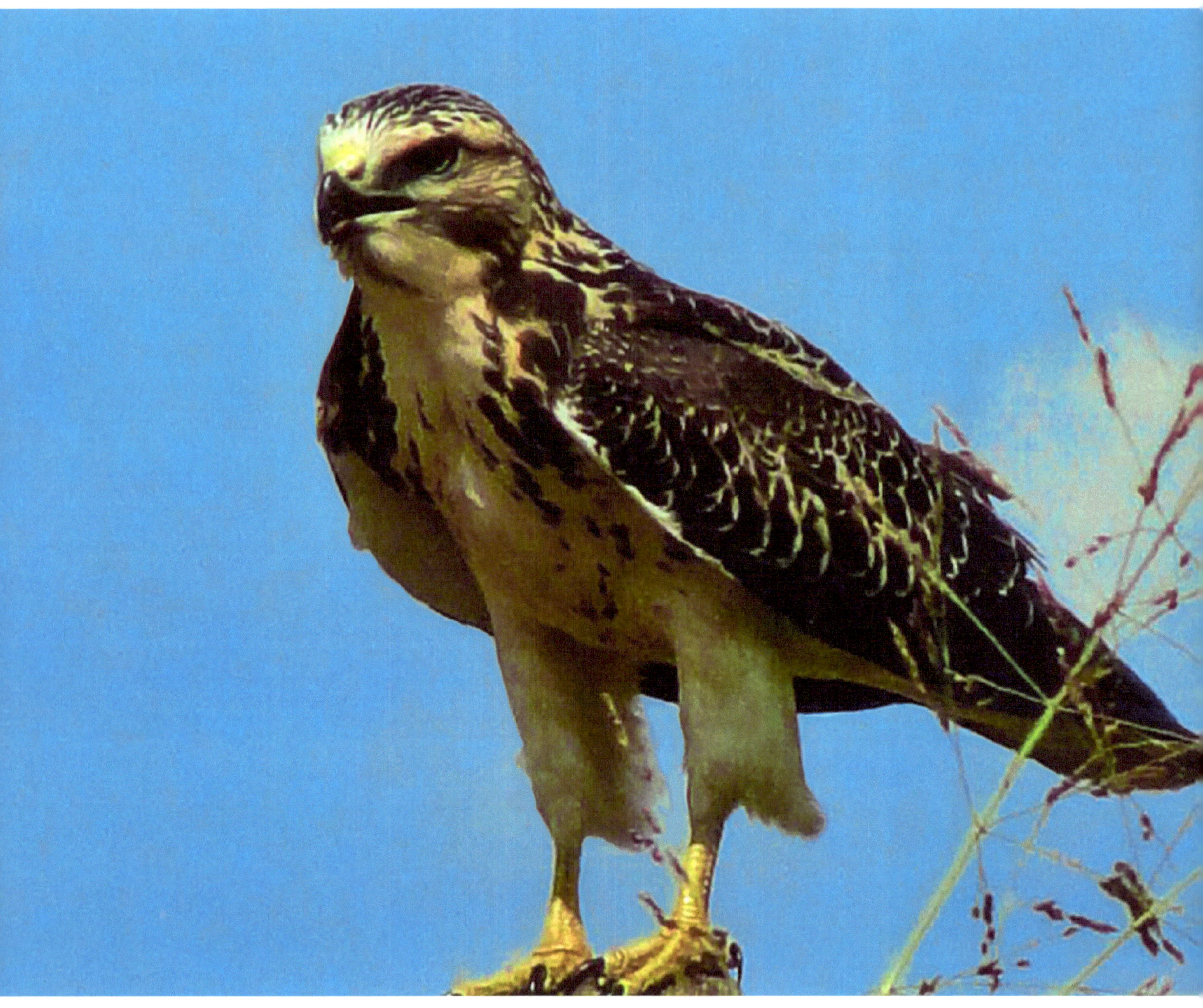

Hawk, Kansas (Mark Pendergrass)

Drape the hill that for centuries changed not at all.
In the summery sky the hawk shrills out her call,

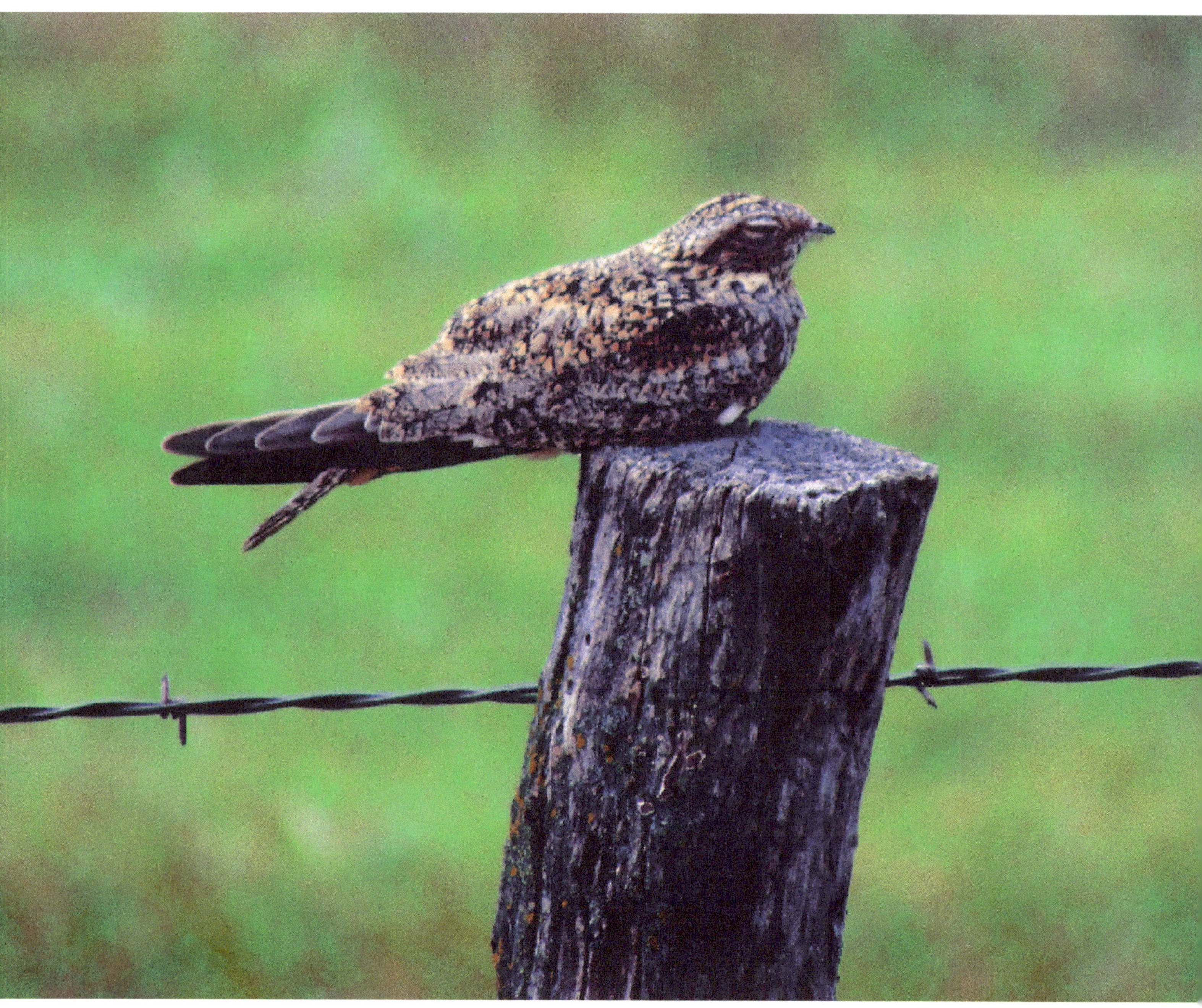

Whippoorwill, Kansas (Mark Pendergrass)

And the whippoorwills cry in the soft evening air,
As their ancestors did, when the people were there.

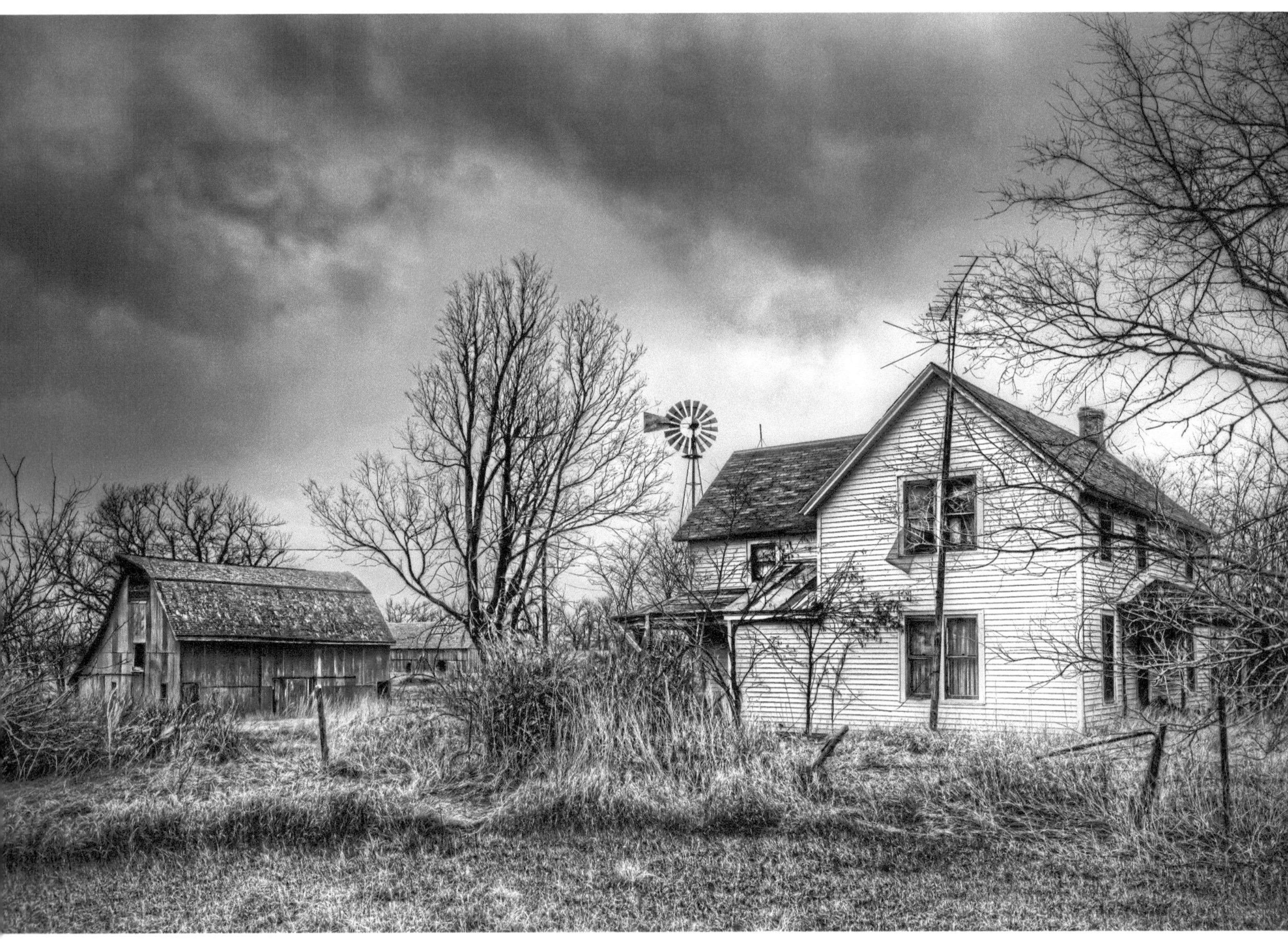

Ghost house, Ellsworth #4 (Dave McKane)

So consider these lines; please don't toss them aside,

For herein lies a truth about man and his pride:

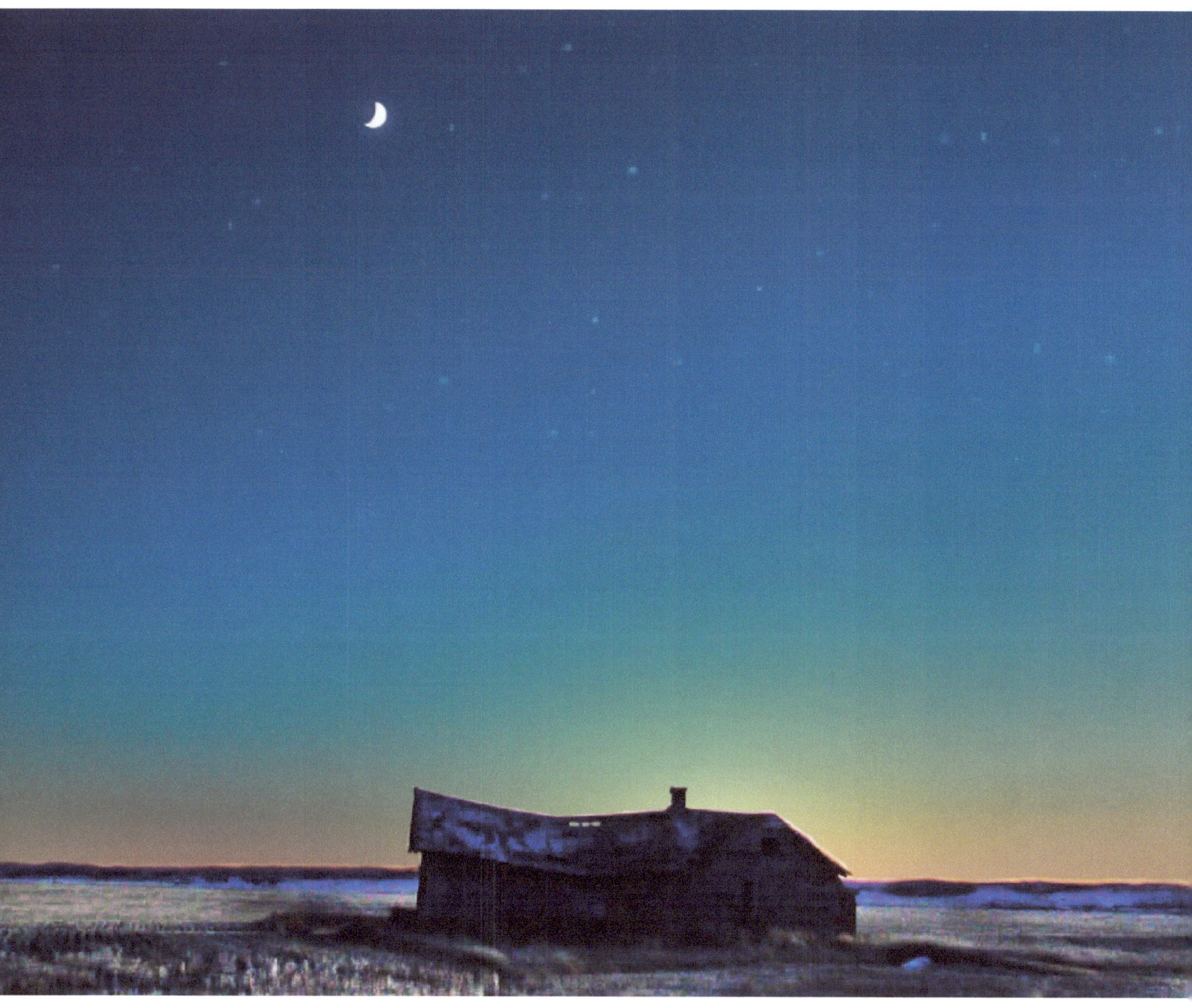

Big prairie sky, Saskatchewan (Cris Sia Moresca)

Very transient, at best, are the works of man's hand,
But the works of his Maker forever will stand.

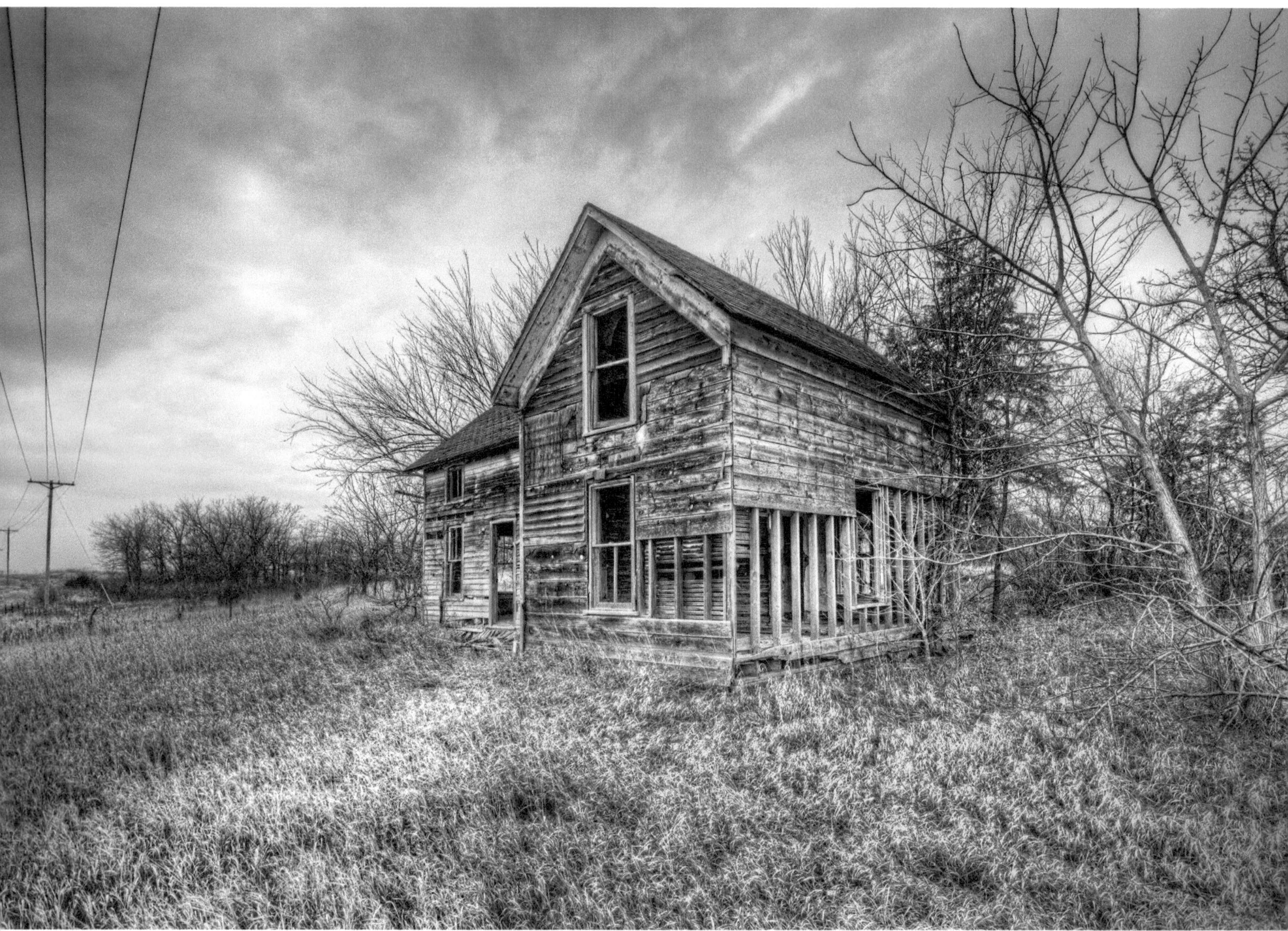

Ghost house, Fairview, Kansas (Dave McKane)

Put your faith in the things that will be there always;
Value not, to excess, what must end in decay.

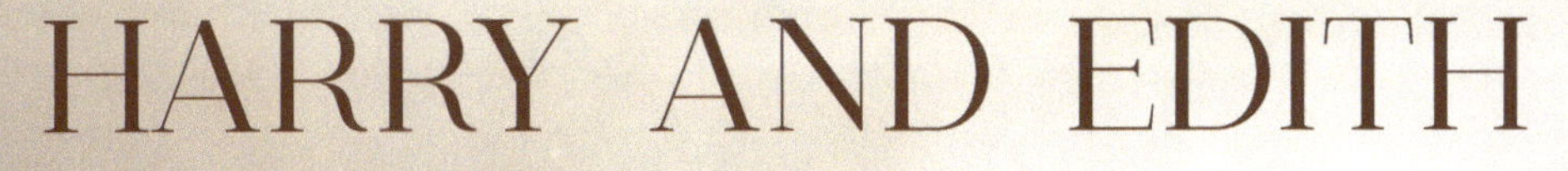

III.

HARRY AND EDITH
(A PRAIRIE TALE)

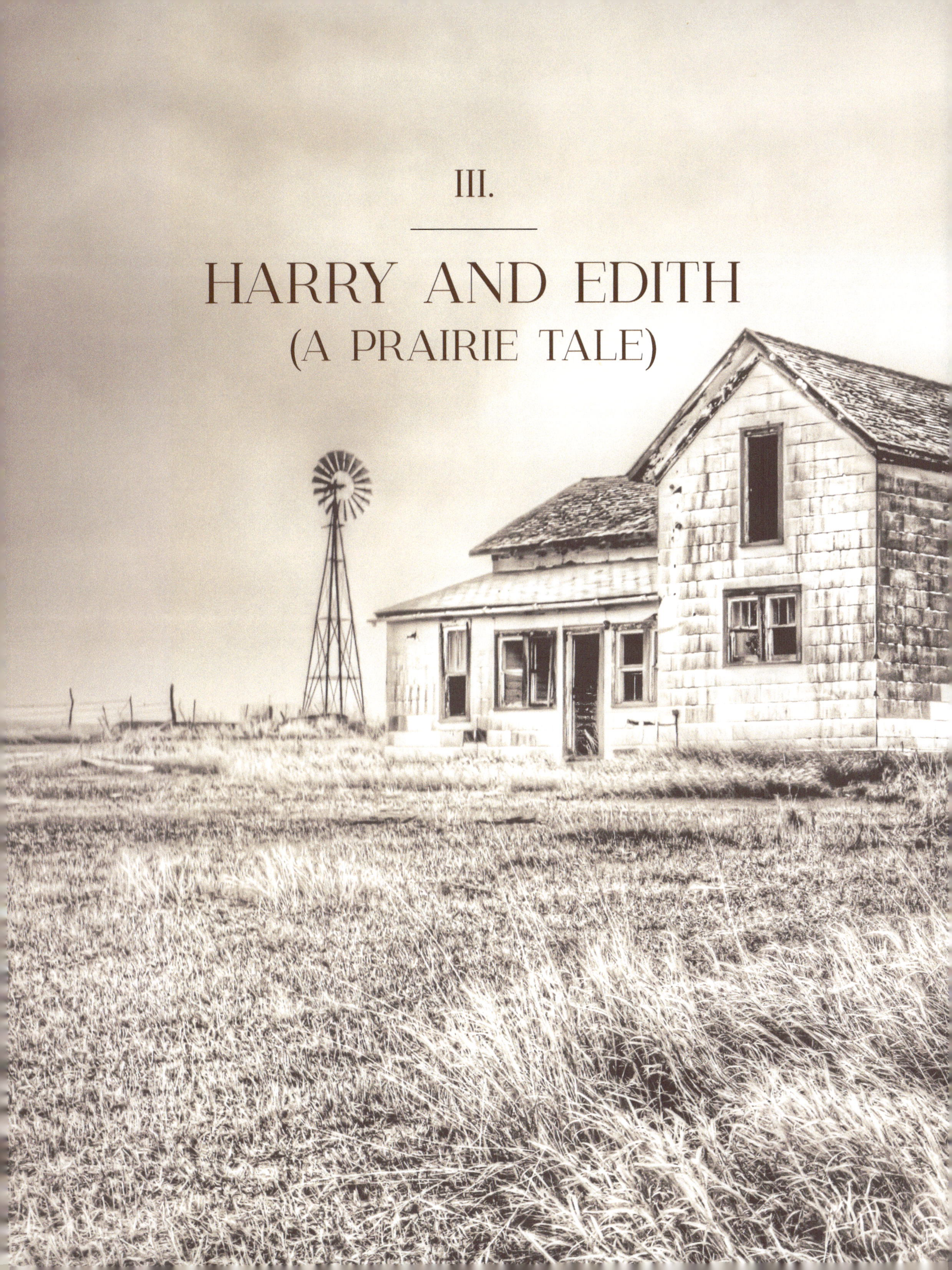

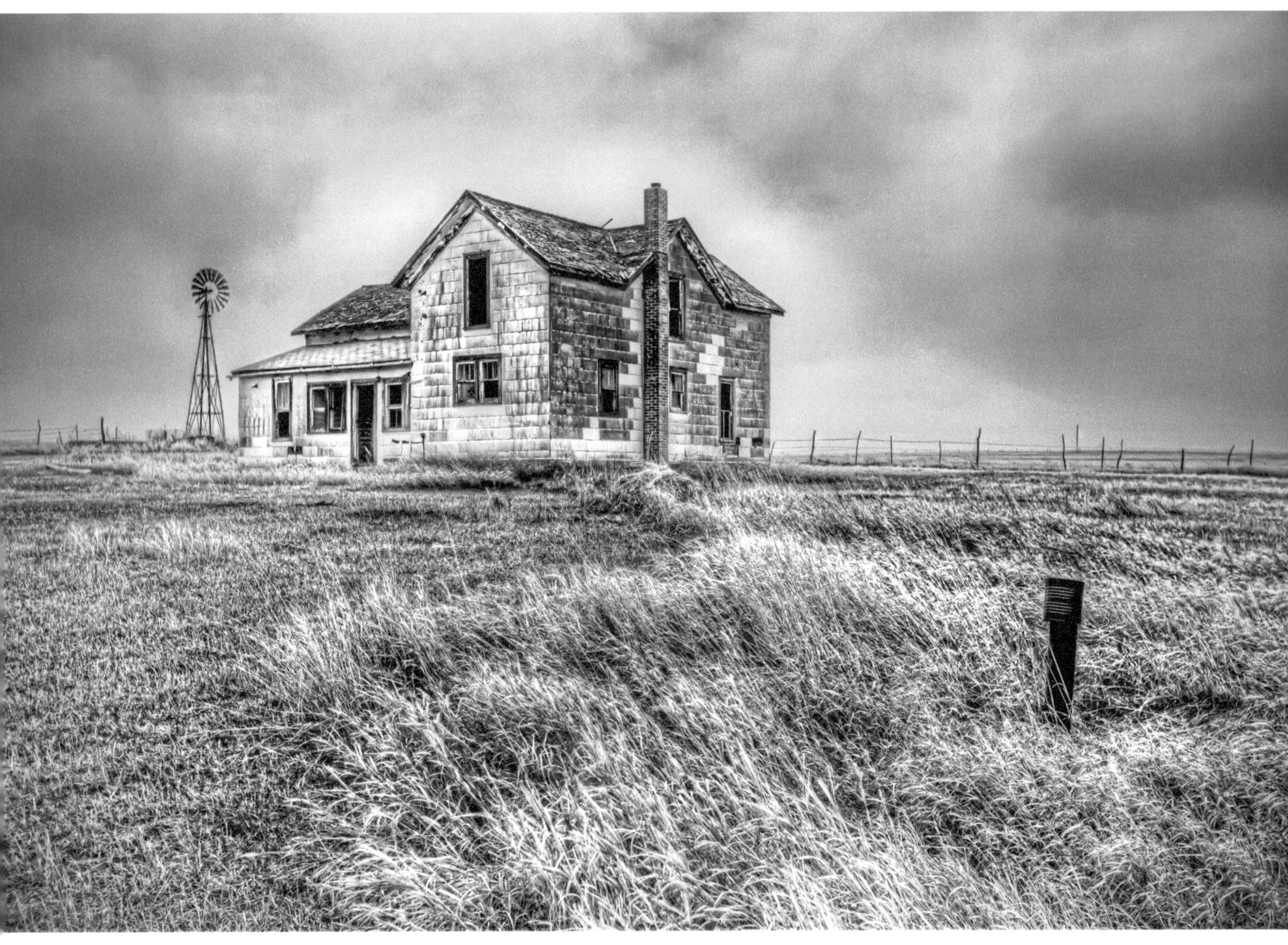

Ghost house, Ellsworth #10, Kansas (Dave McKane)

There a family once lived, wresting life from the soil—
Just a meager subsistence, despite all their toil.

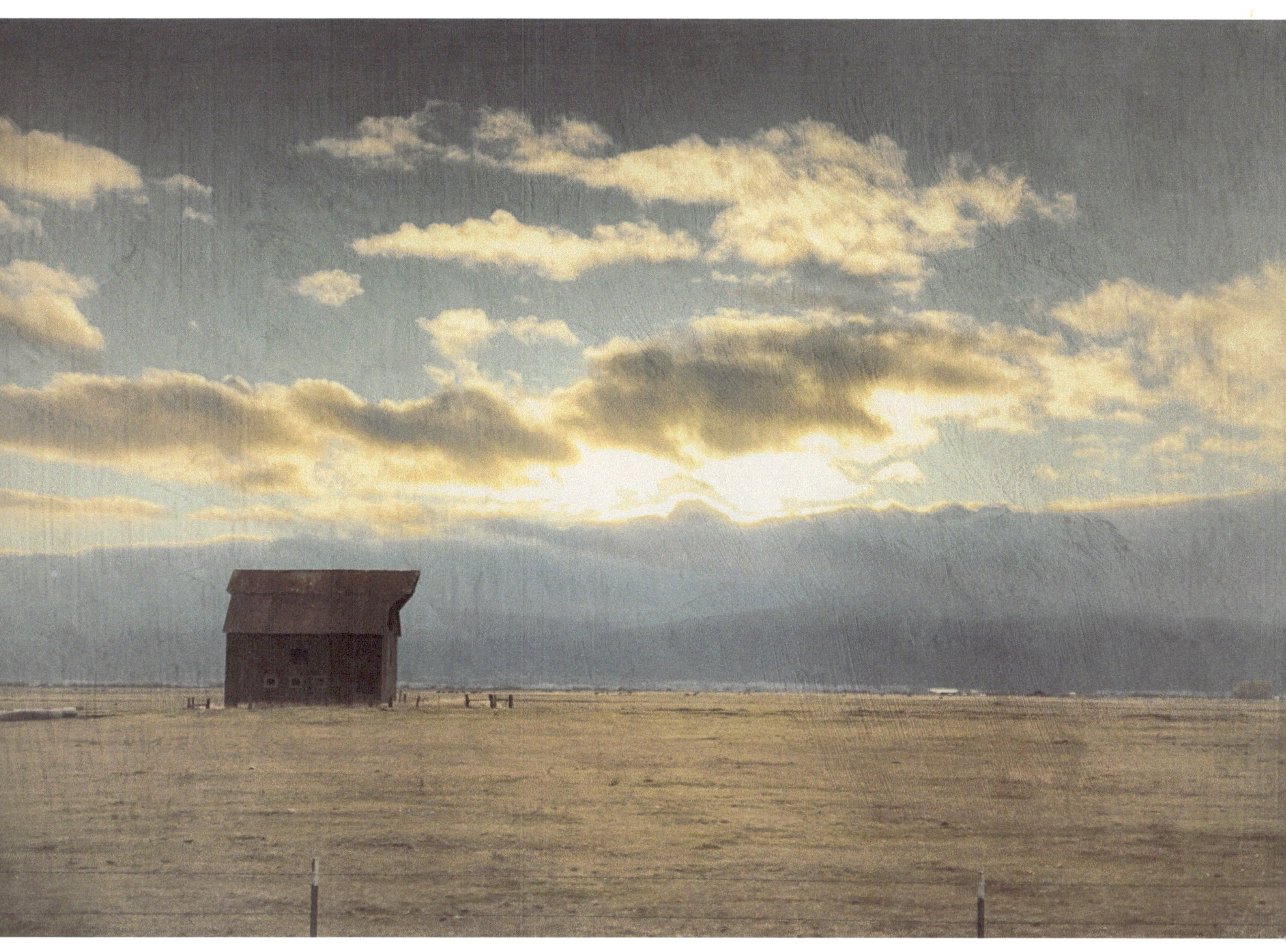

Drought (Mark Murphy)

There were sicknesses, bills, also floods o'er the fields,
And at other times drought did diminish their yields . . .

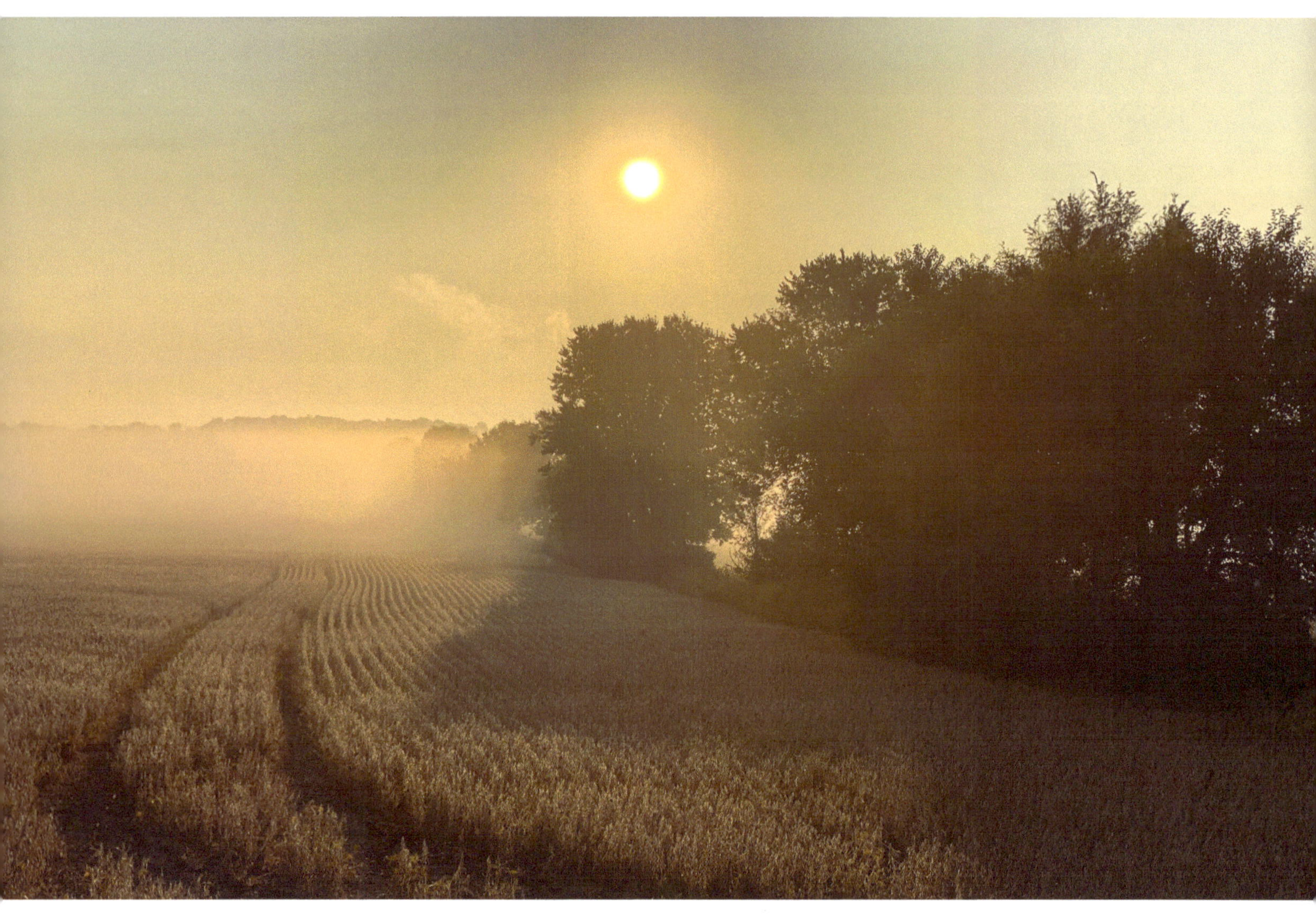

Brutal summer heat (Mark Murphy)

Not to mention the boulders and stumps to be found,
And the ravenous insects infesting the ground.

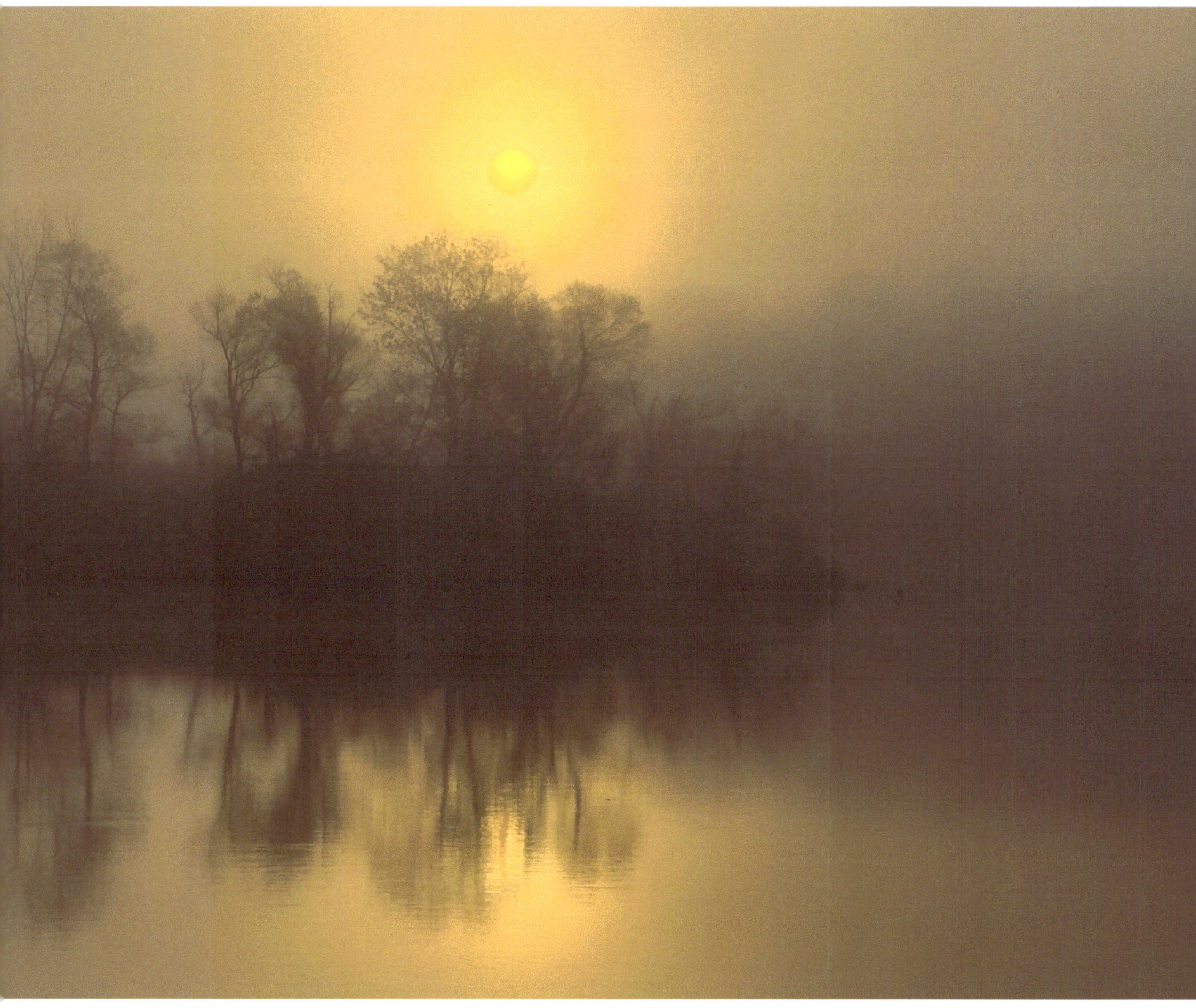

Fog over lake (Mark Murphy)

Well, the years slowly passed, but the times got no better:
One son goes to war; off to college, the other.

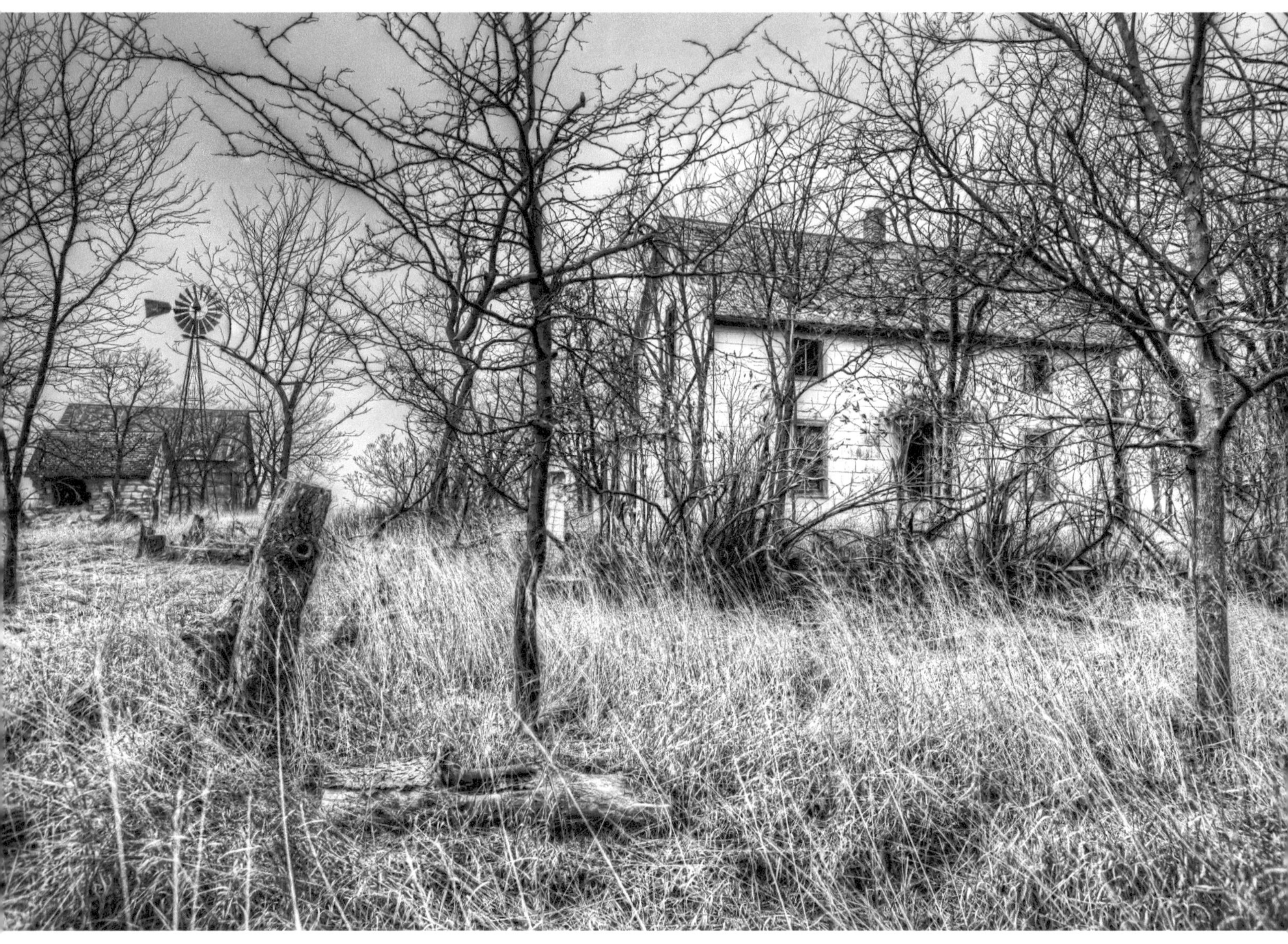

Ghost house, Ellsworth #11, Kansas (Dave McKane)

The aged granddad was laid up with a stroke;
All alone now, the parents redoubled their work.

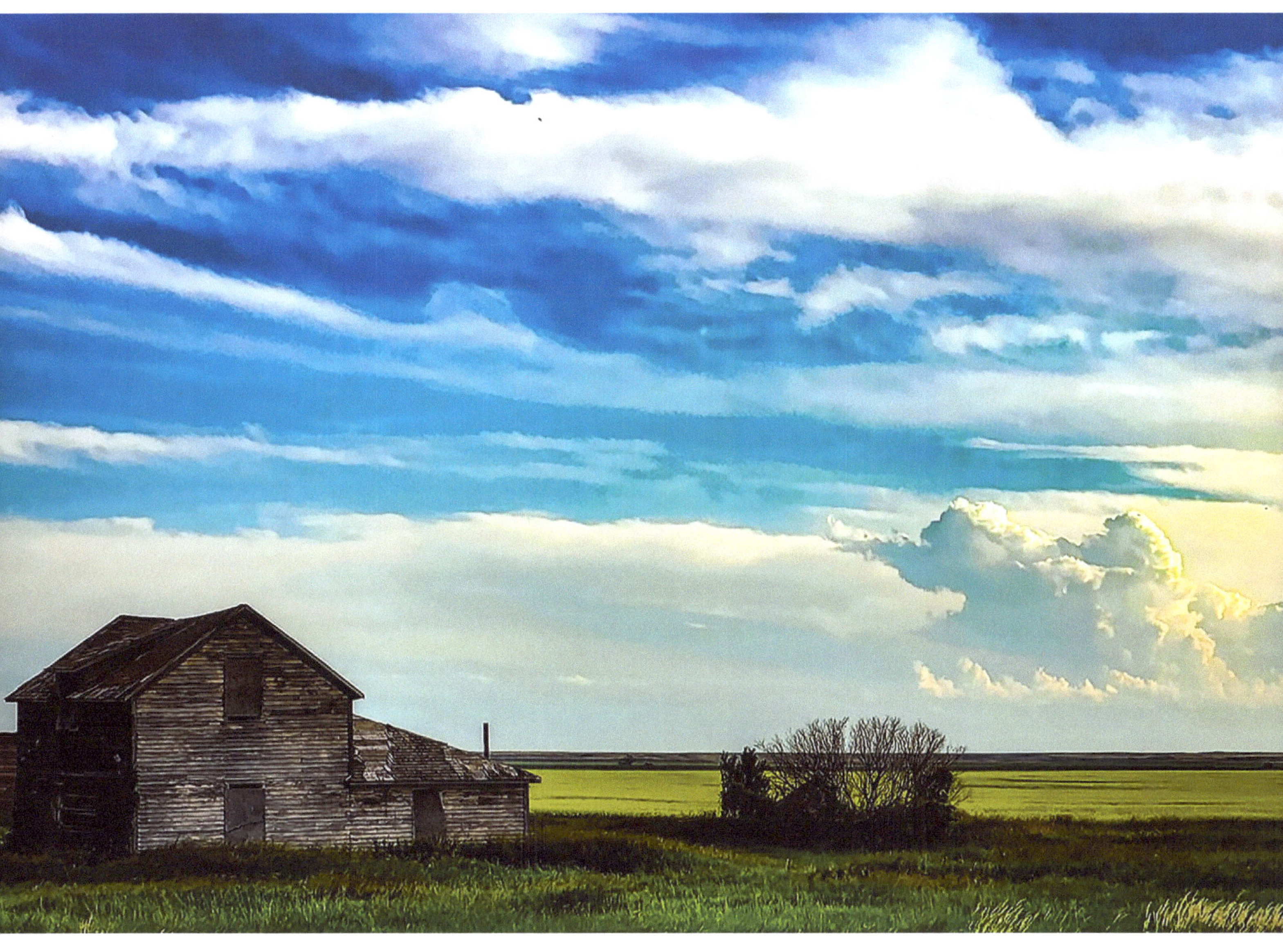

Storm coming, Saskatchewan (Cris Sia Moresca)

When the day fin'lly came that their toils were all through,
Their estate, auctioned off, scarcely paid what was due.

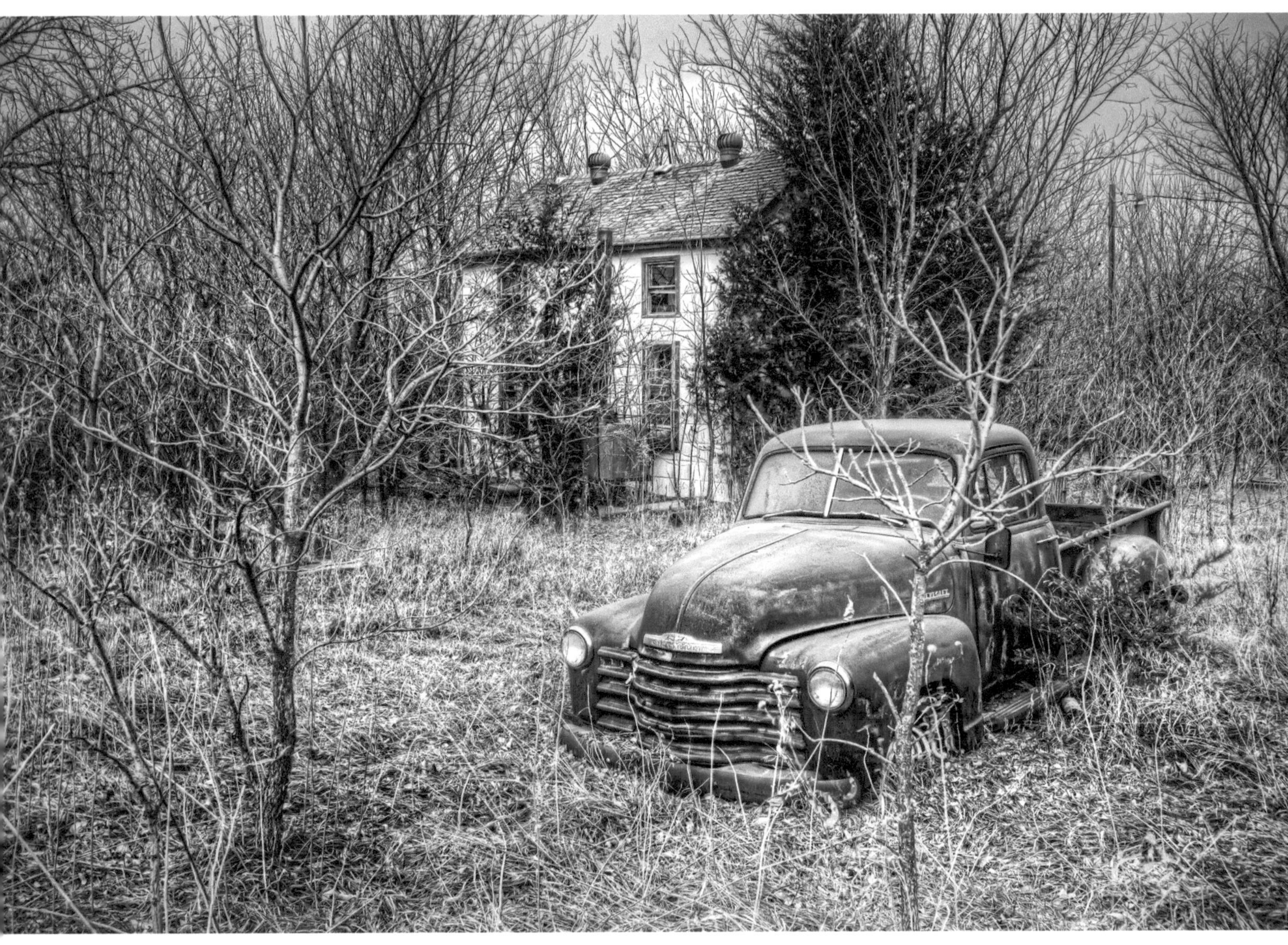

Ghost house and Chevy truck, Quenemo #1, Kansas (Dave McKane)

Yet the heritage left was a rich one indeed:
An untarnished name was their 'queath, 'twas agreed.

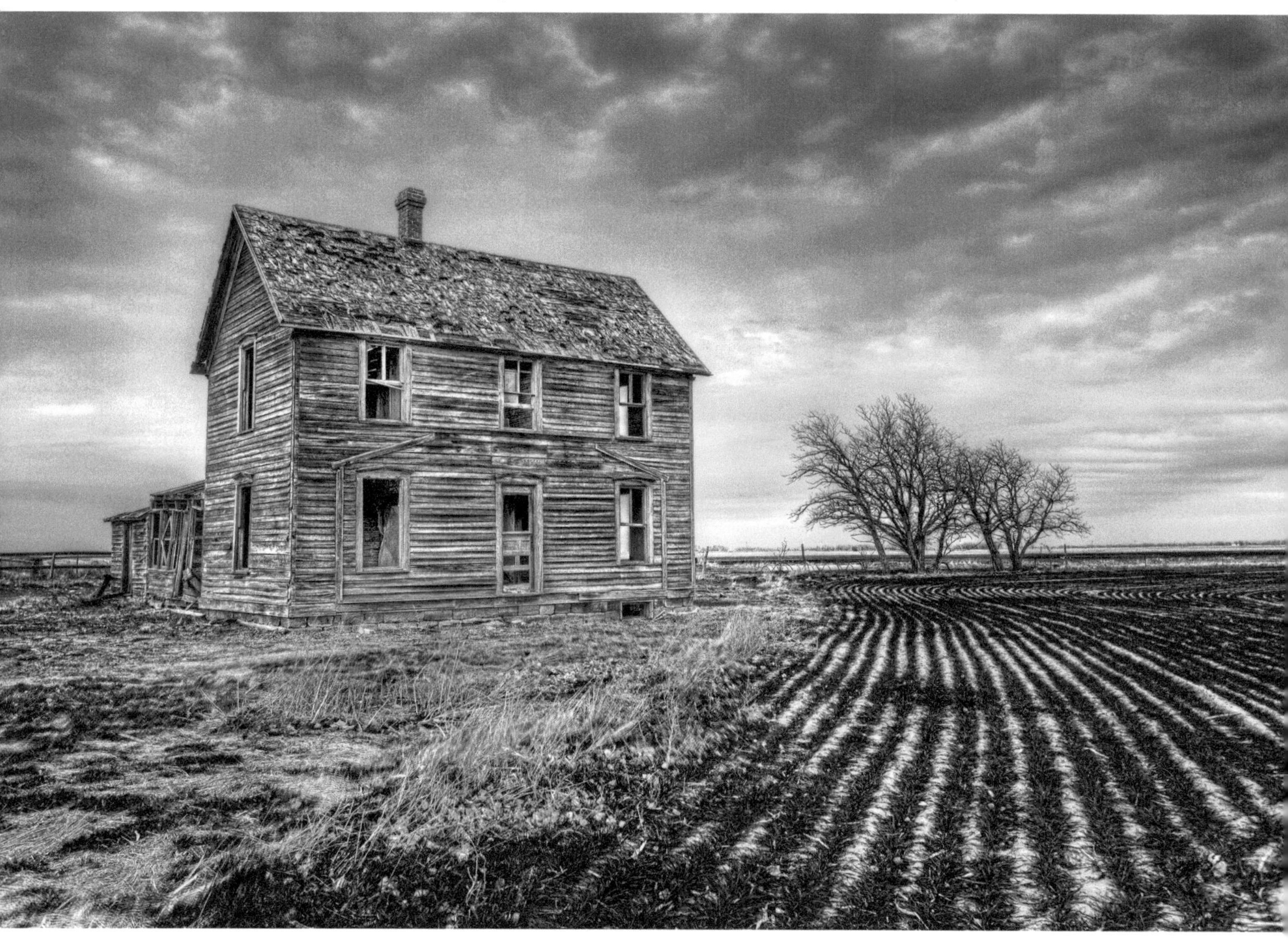

Ghost house, Dodge City #2, Kansas (Dave McKane)

They were known near and far for their neighborly ways
And some old-fashioned principles gracing their days.

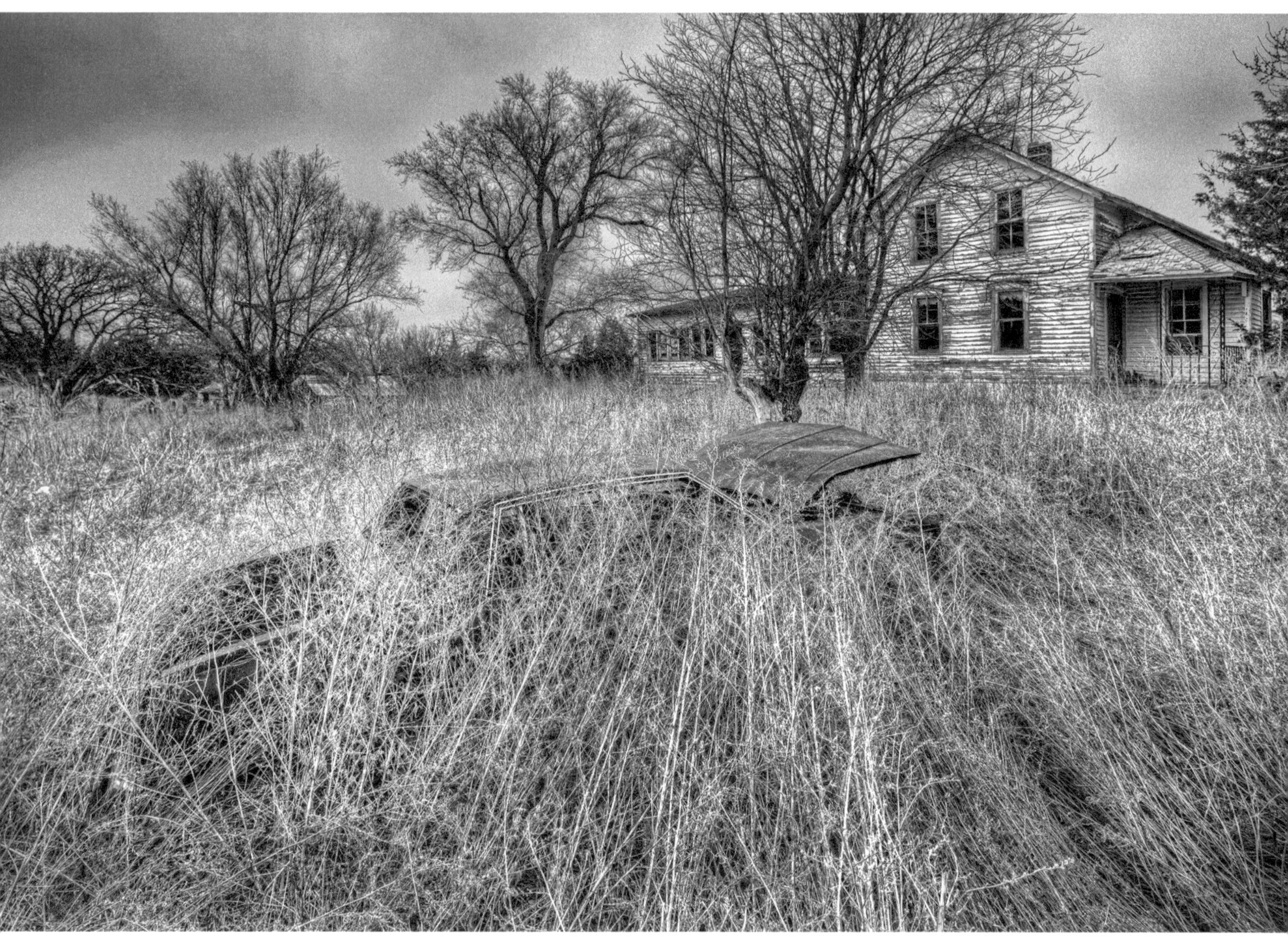

Ghost house, Downs #2, Kansas (Dave McKane)

Also, four kids grew up to start homes of their own
That reflected the values their parents had known.

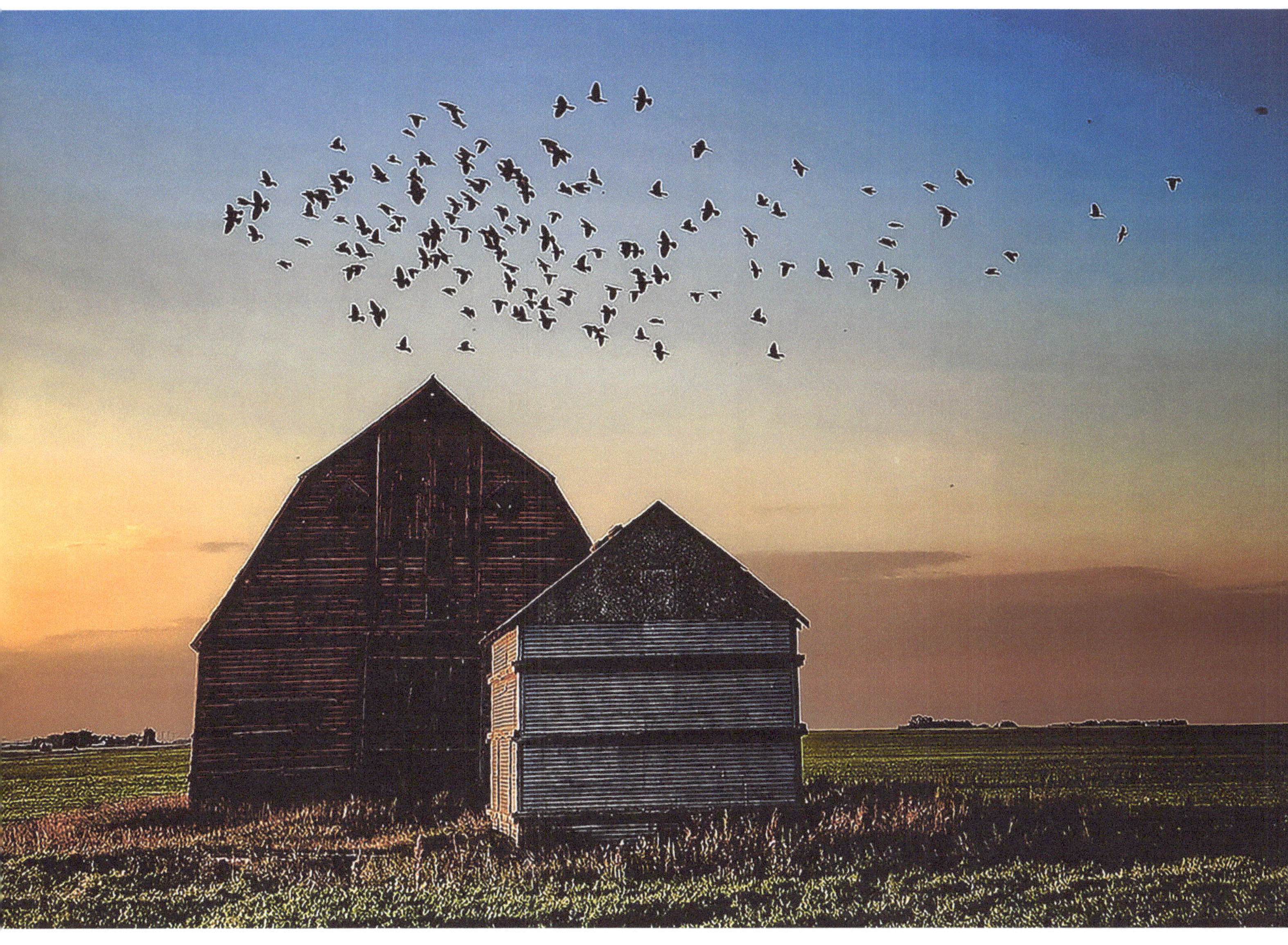

Barns and birds, Saskatchewan (Cris Sia Moresca)

They were plain country folks without pretense or guile,
With some quaint country ways that might prompt a wry smile.

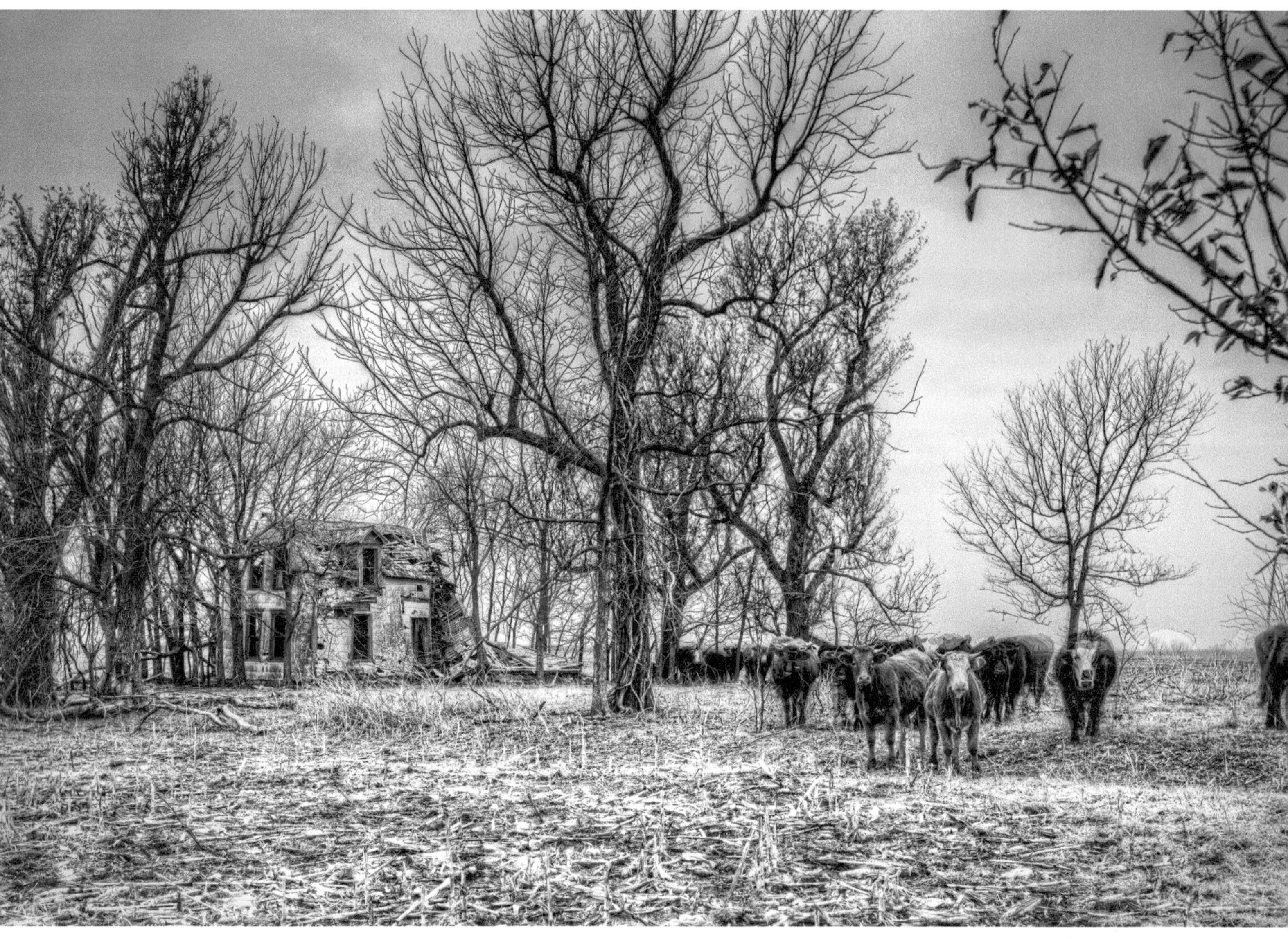

Ghost house, Effingham, Kansas (Dave McKane)

Honest work and fair dealings were ever the rule,
And a faith that sustained them when fortunes were cruel.

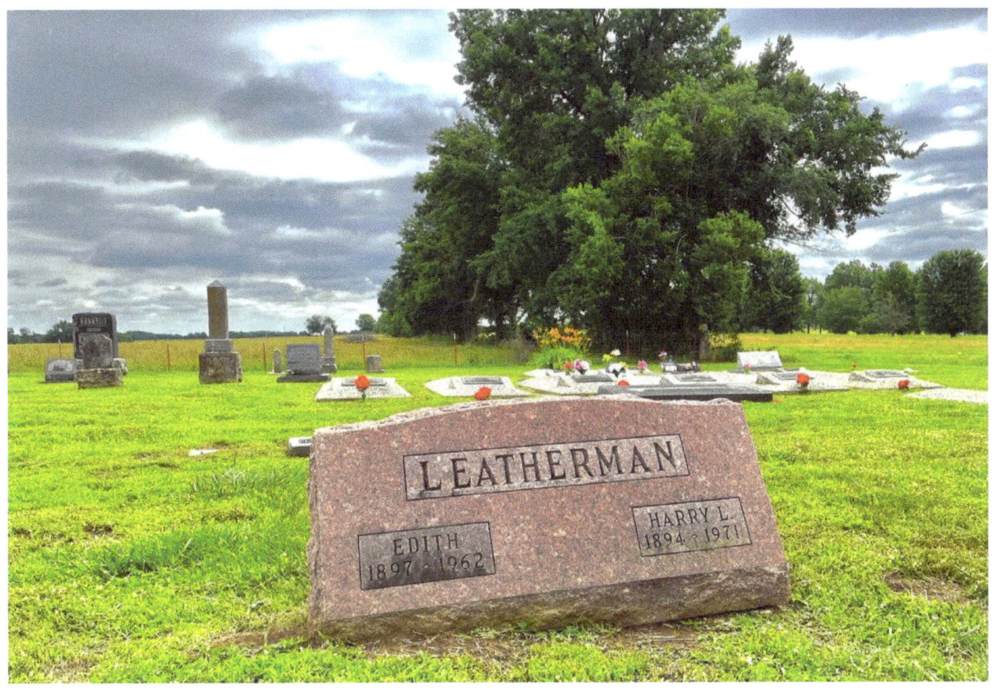

Harry and Edith's headstone, McKill Cemetery, Vernon County, Missouri, 2024 (Lyndell Leatherman)

They died as they lived: self-reliant and free.

Not a bad way to go, just betwixt you and me!

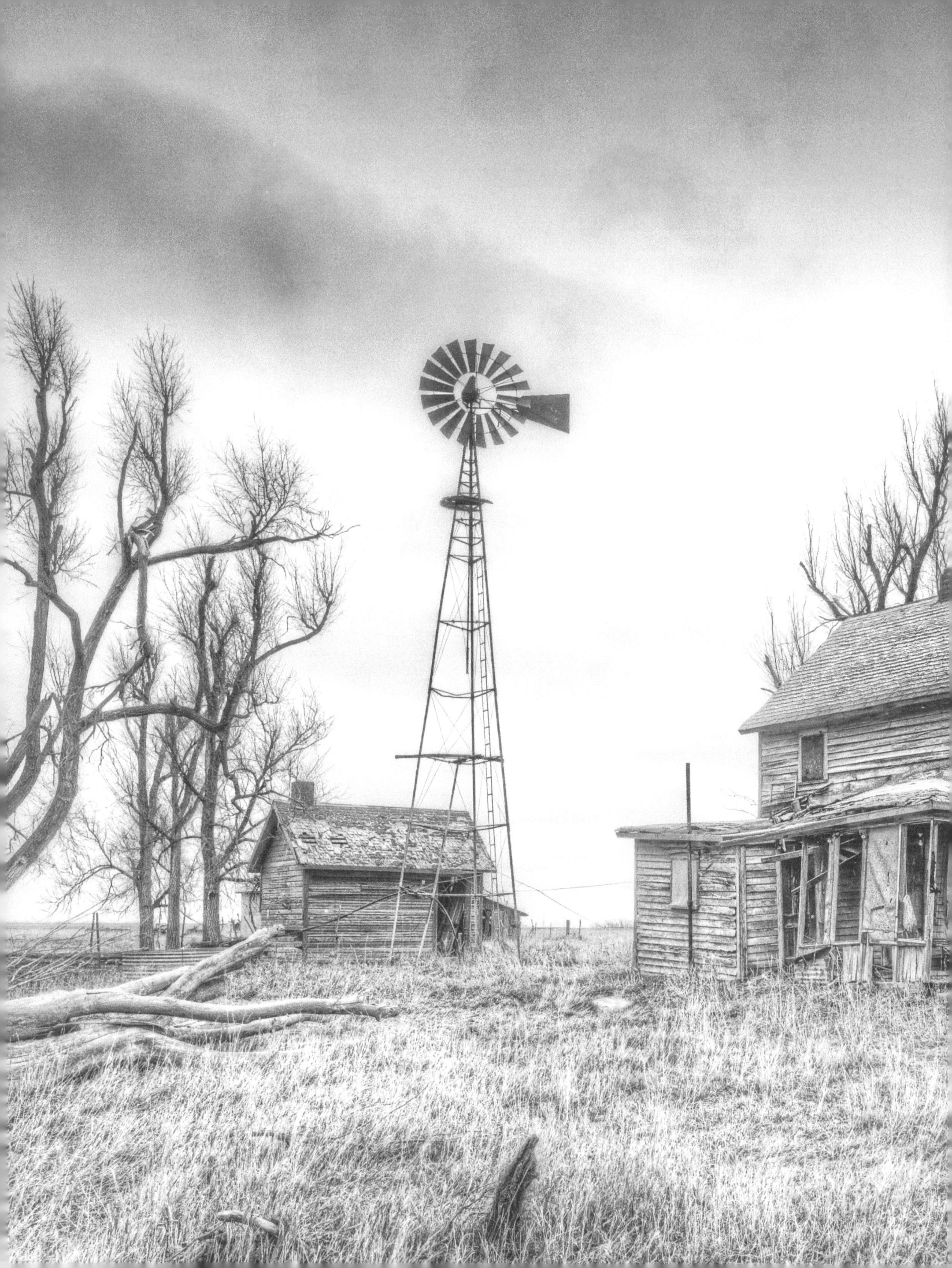

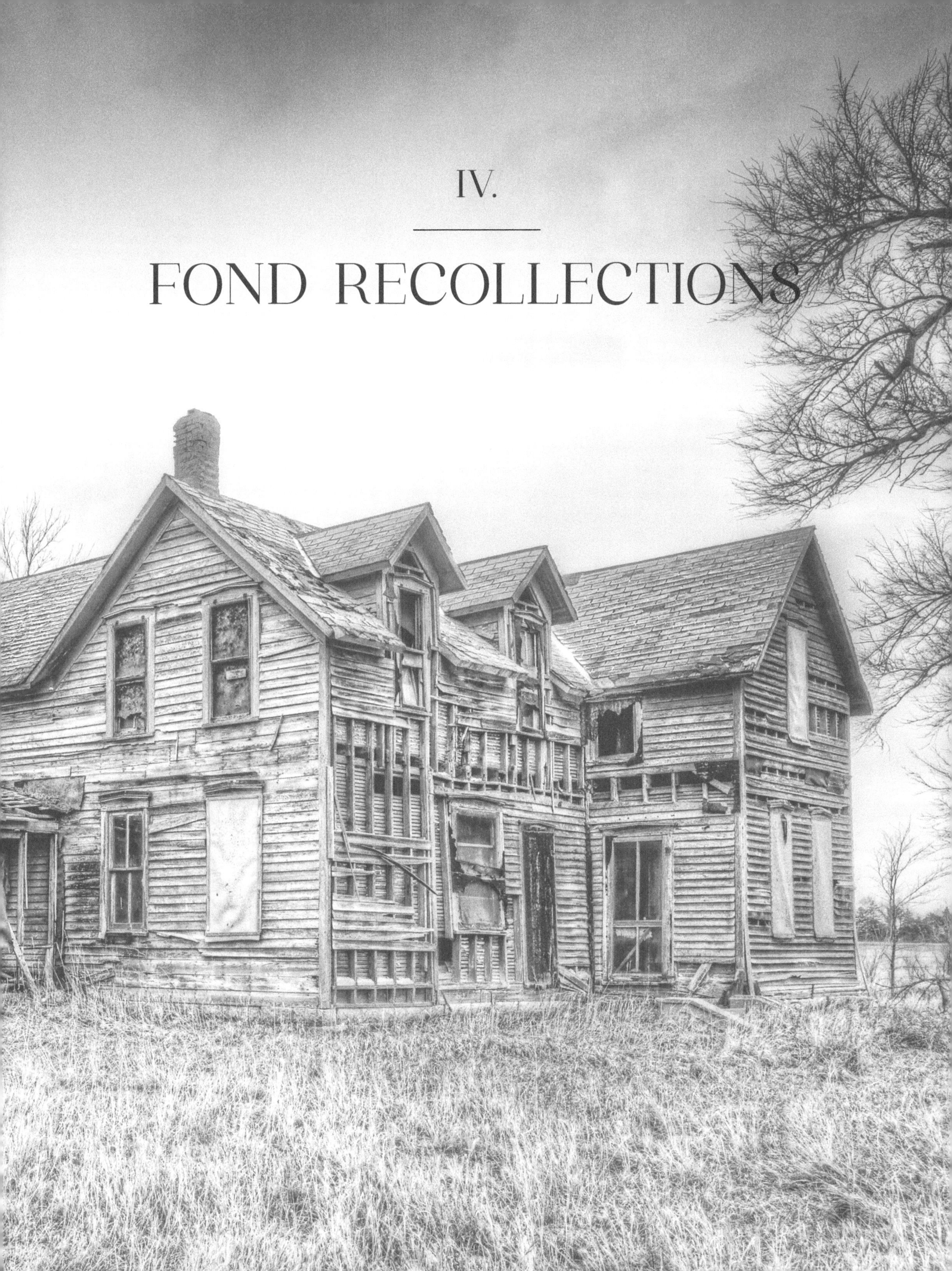

IV.

FOND RECOLLECTIONS

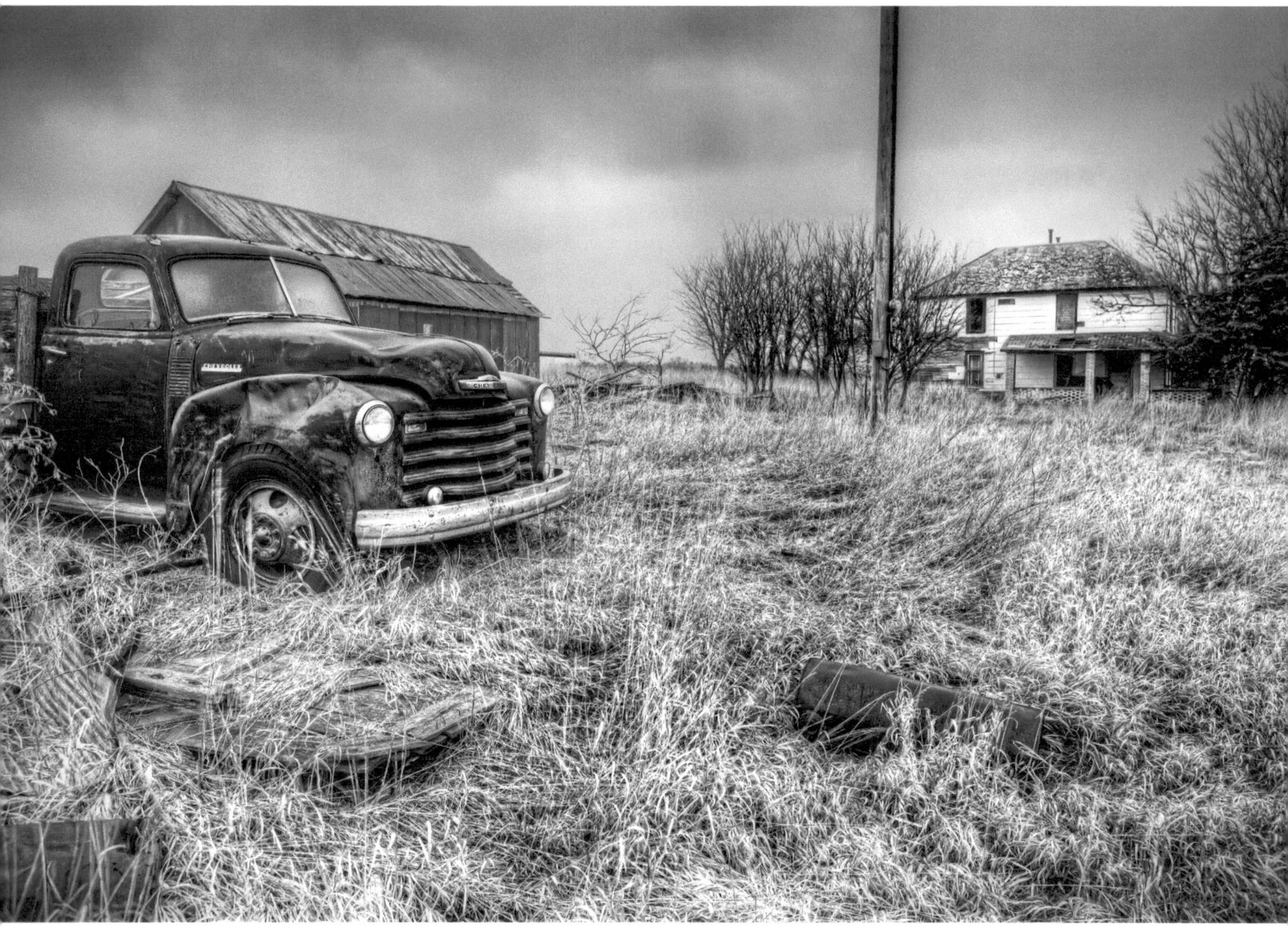

Ghost house, Ellsworth #8, Kansas (Dave McKane)

O'er countless miles and mounting years
Recurring mem'ries come a-winging

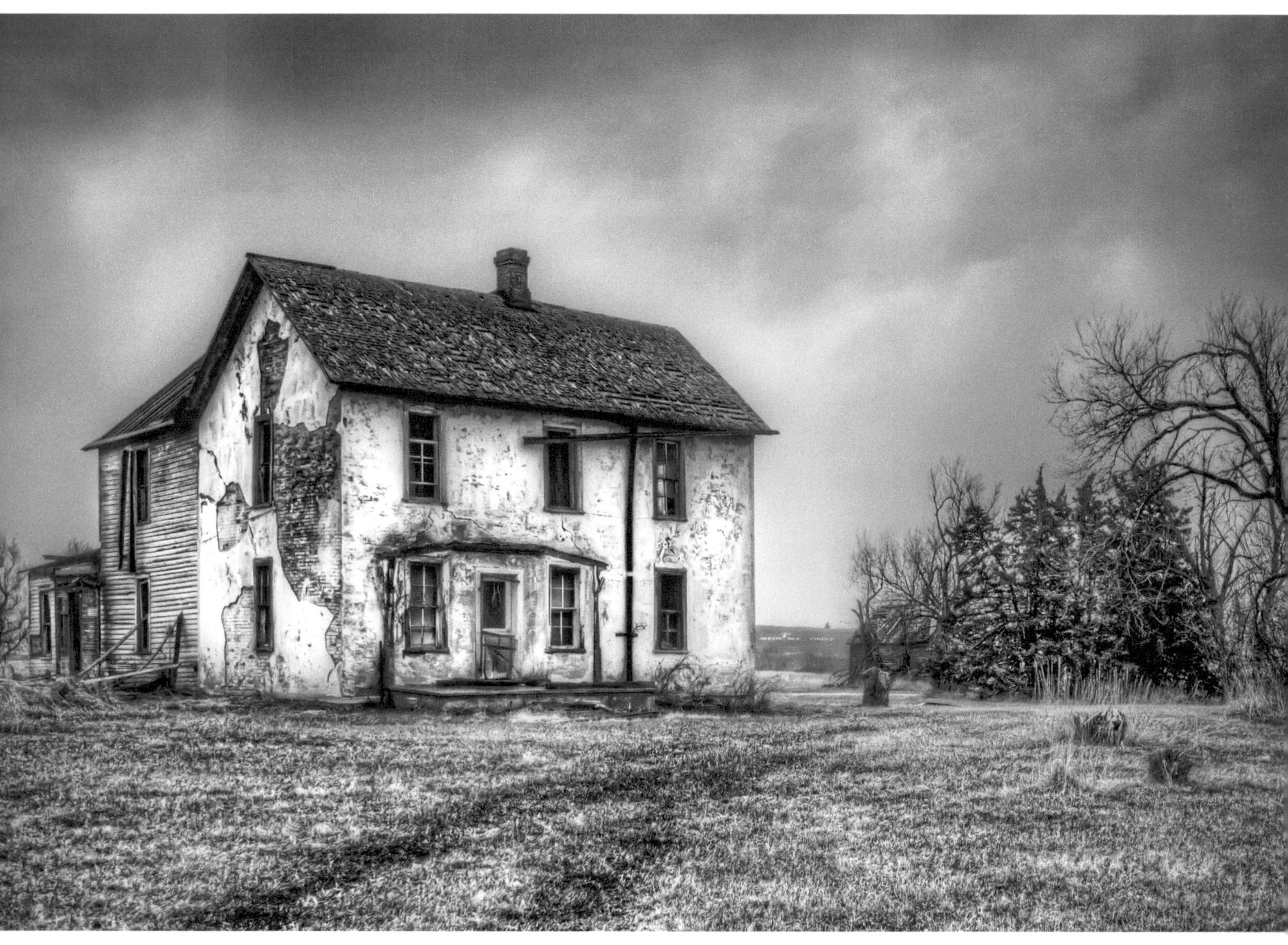

Ghost house, Ellsworth #9, Kansas (Dave McKane)

Which prick the heart and taunt the mind
And linger on as if in teasing.

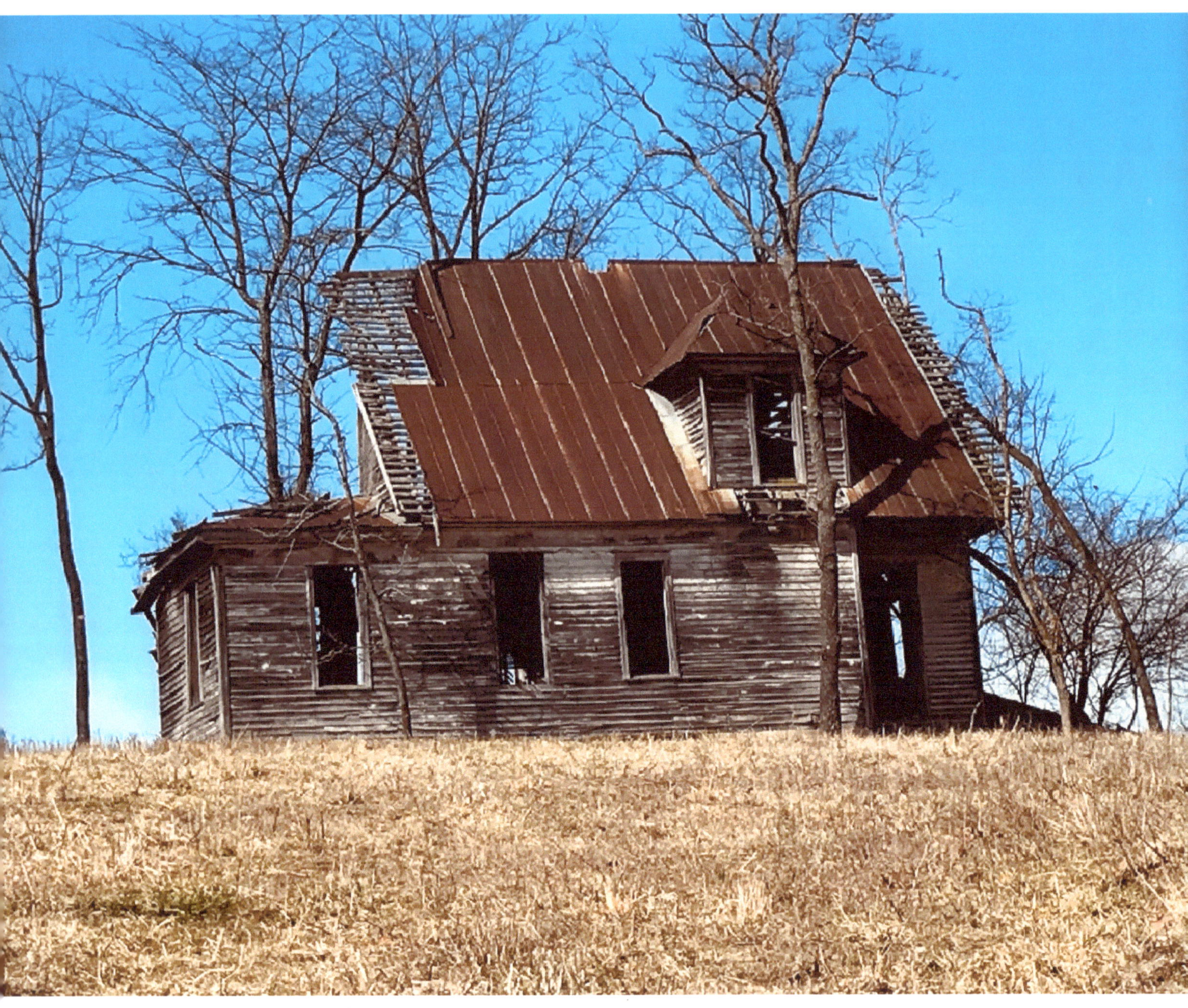

Abandoned Amish house, Seymour, Missouri (Mary Chew)

Though some bring joy and some, chagrin,

They all are ever part of me:

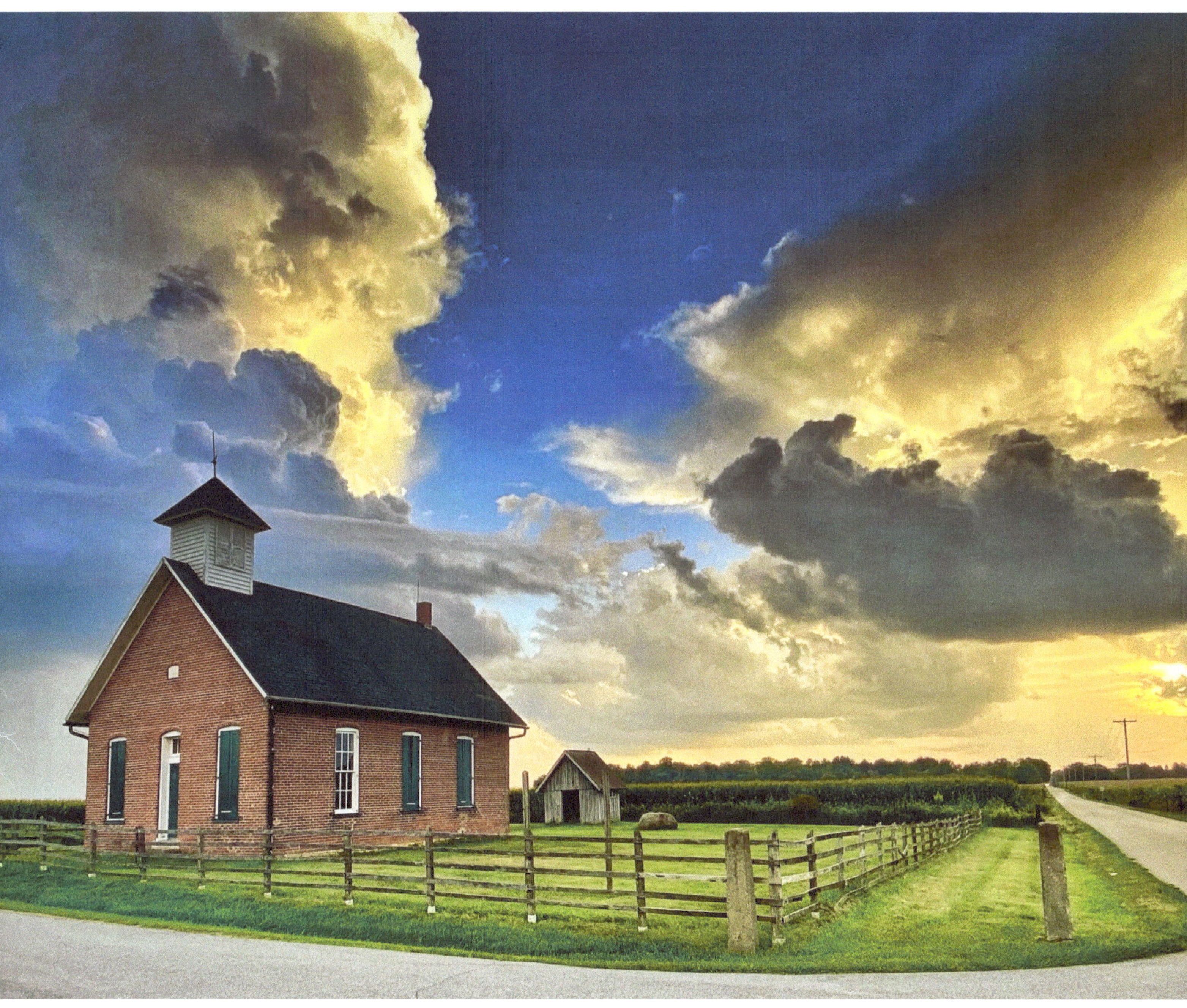

Country school and dramatic clouds (Mark Murphy)

The country church, the one-room school,

The fun and toils of family,

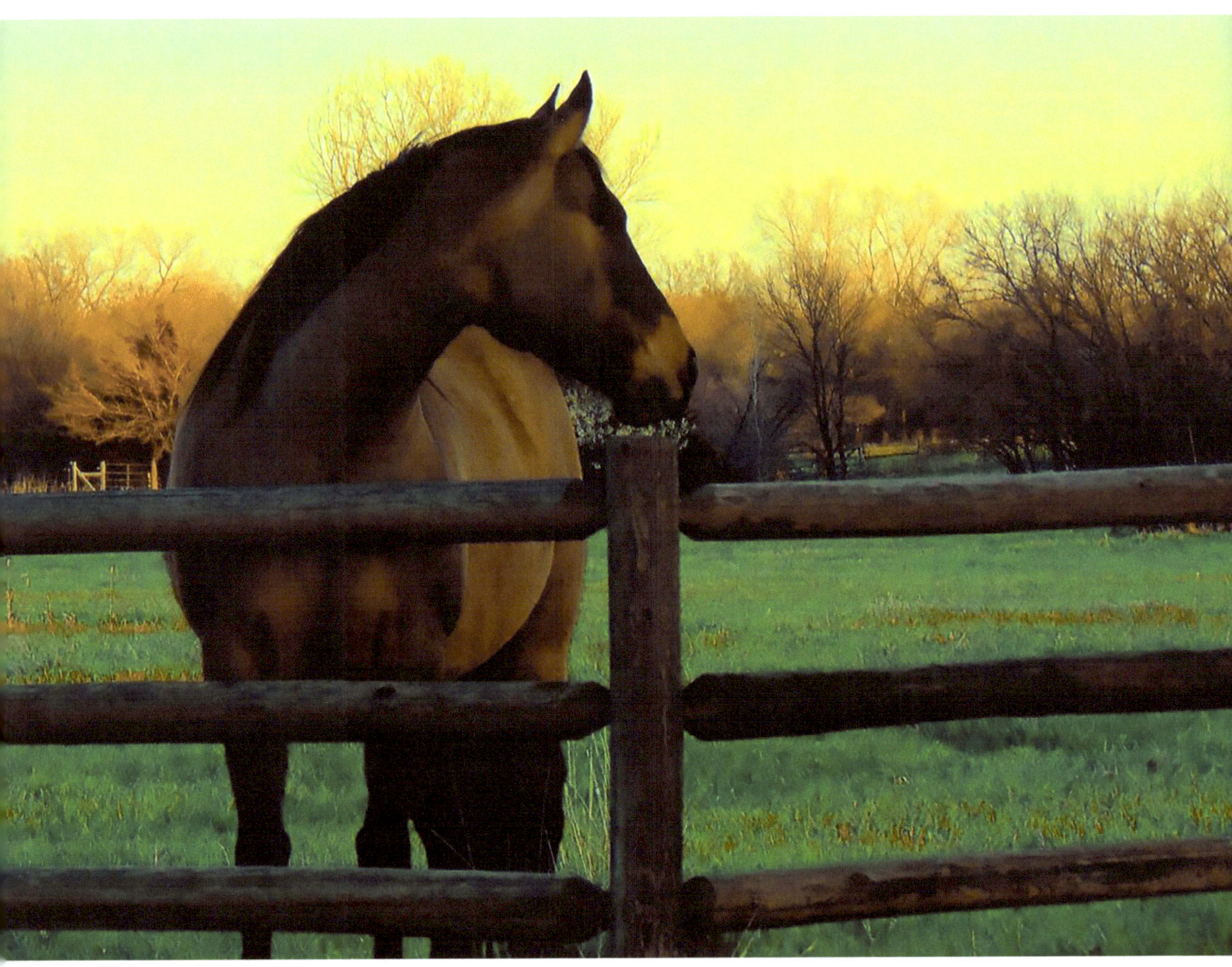

Horse, Kansas (Mark Pendergrass)

My childhood friends and games we played,
The barnyard pets and fields of hay,

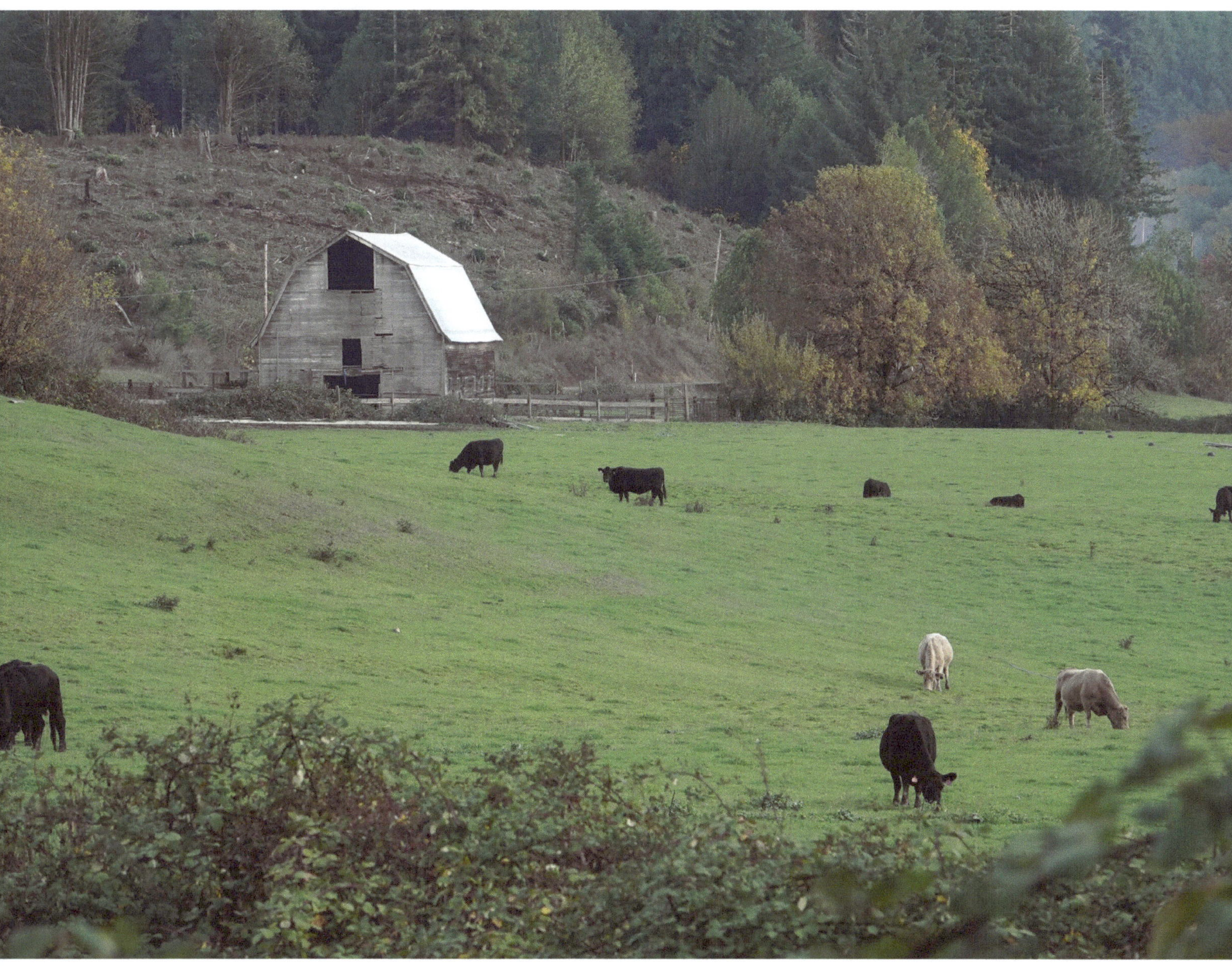

Cattle grazing (Mark Murphy)

The planting time, with hope renewed,
And care of livestock twice a day,

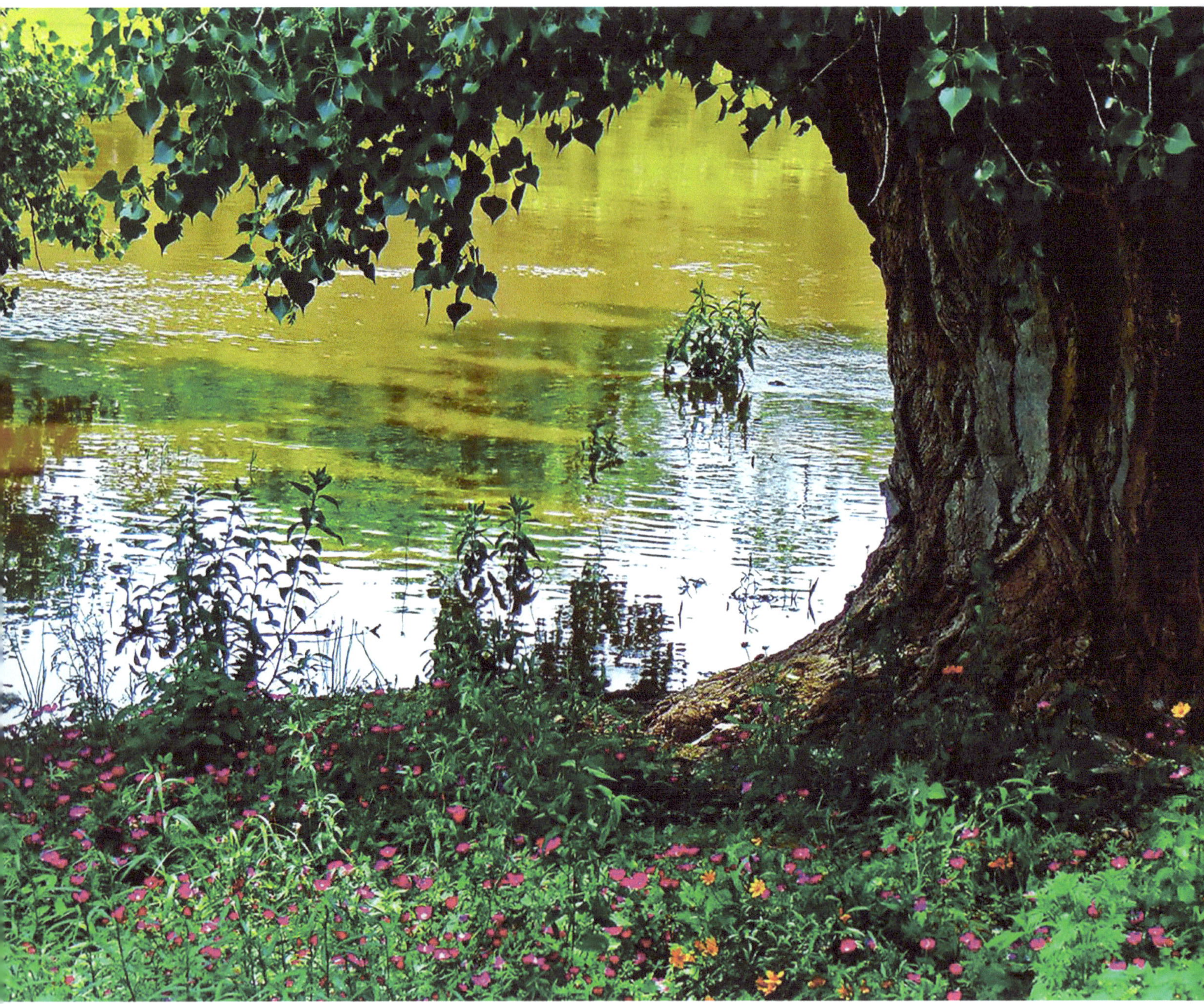

Swimming hole, Kansas (Mark Pendergrass)

Those rented farms, the swimming holes,
Out attic bedroom during storm,

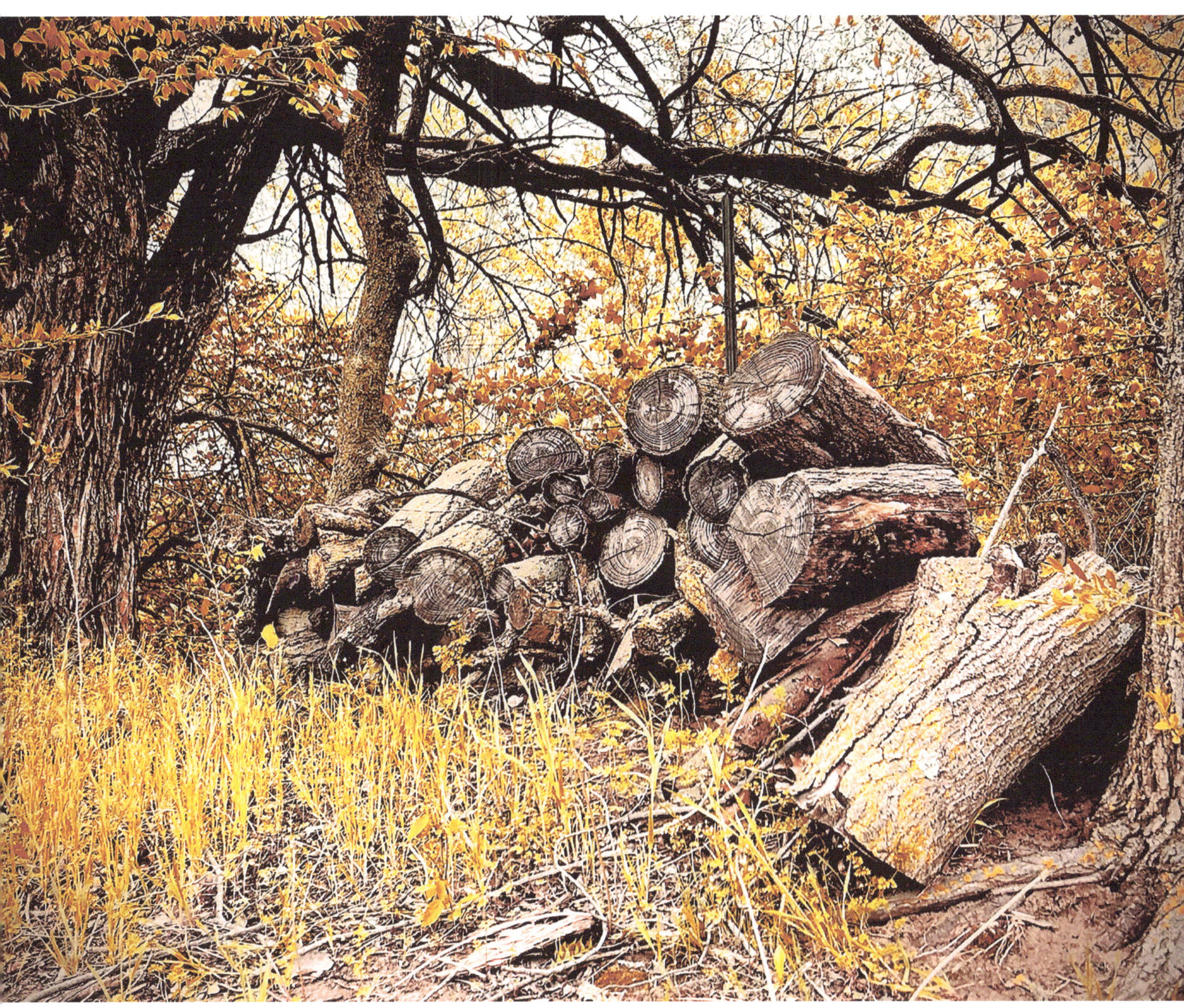

Woodpile, Kansas (Mark Pendergrass)

Supplies of wood and also coal
On winter nights to keep us warm,

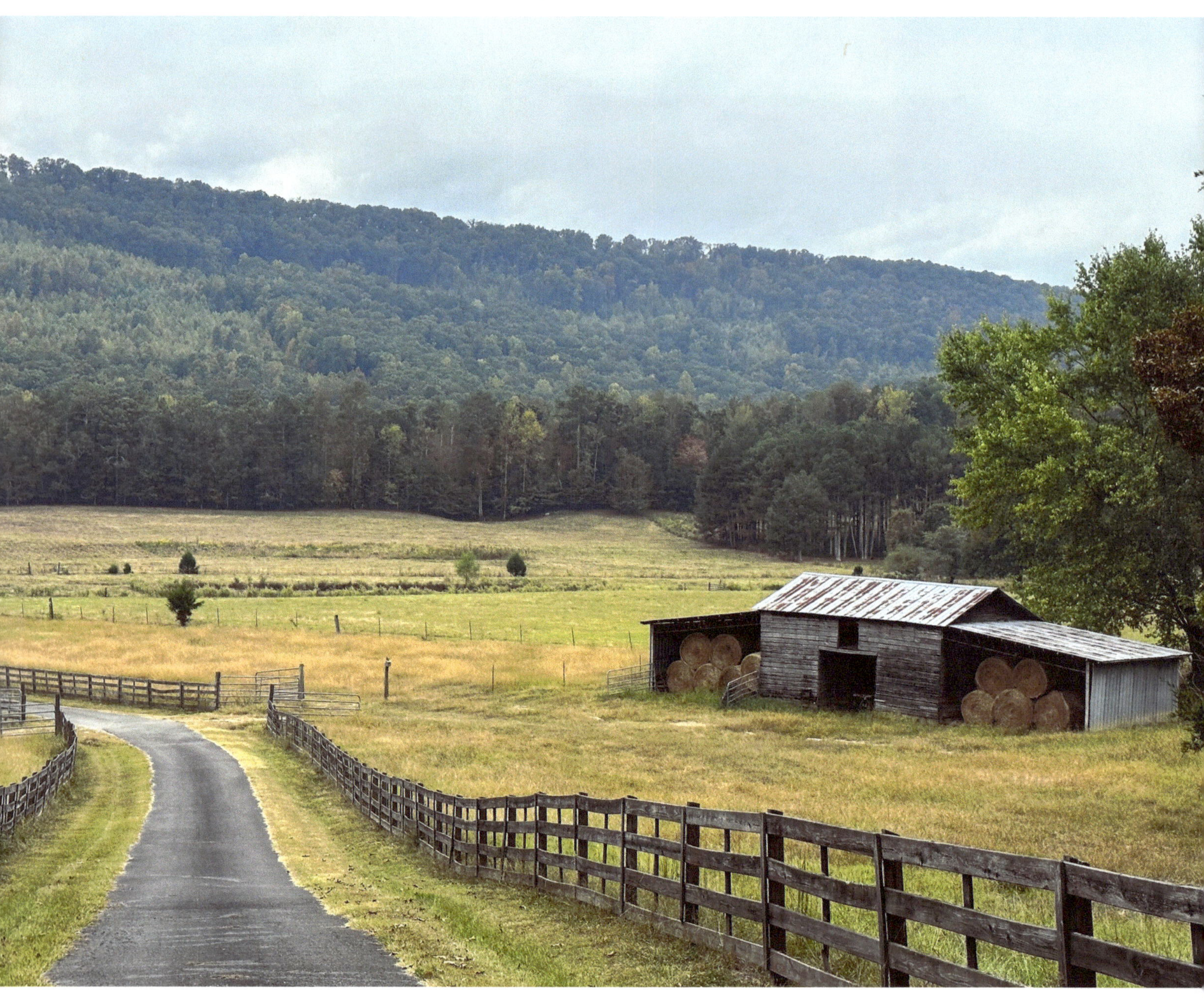

Hay in barn (Mark Murphy)

The harvest days at summer's end
With bulging loft and granary,

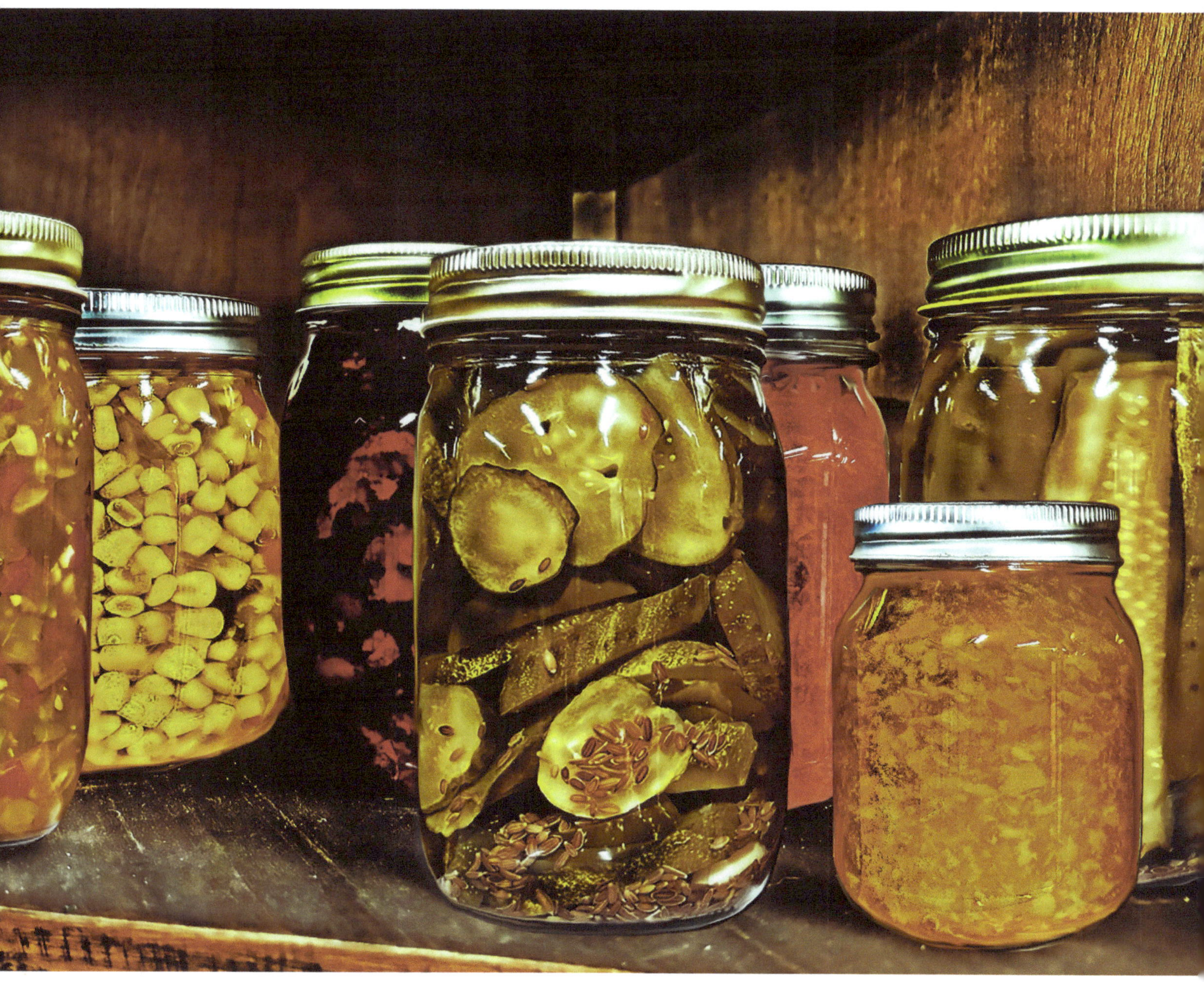

Root cellar produce, Kansas (Mark Pendergrass)

The cellar, jars, and bins replete
With garden produce squirreled away.

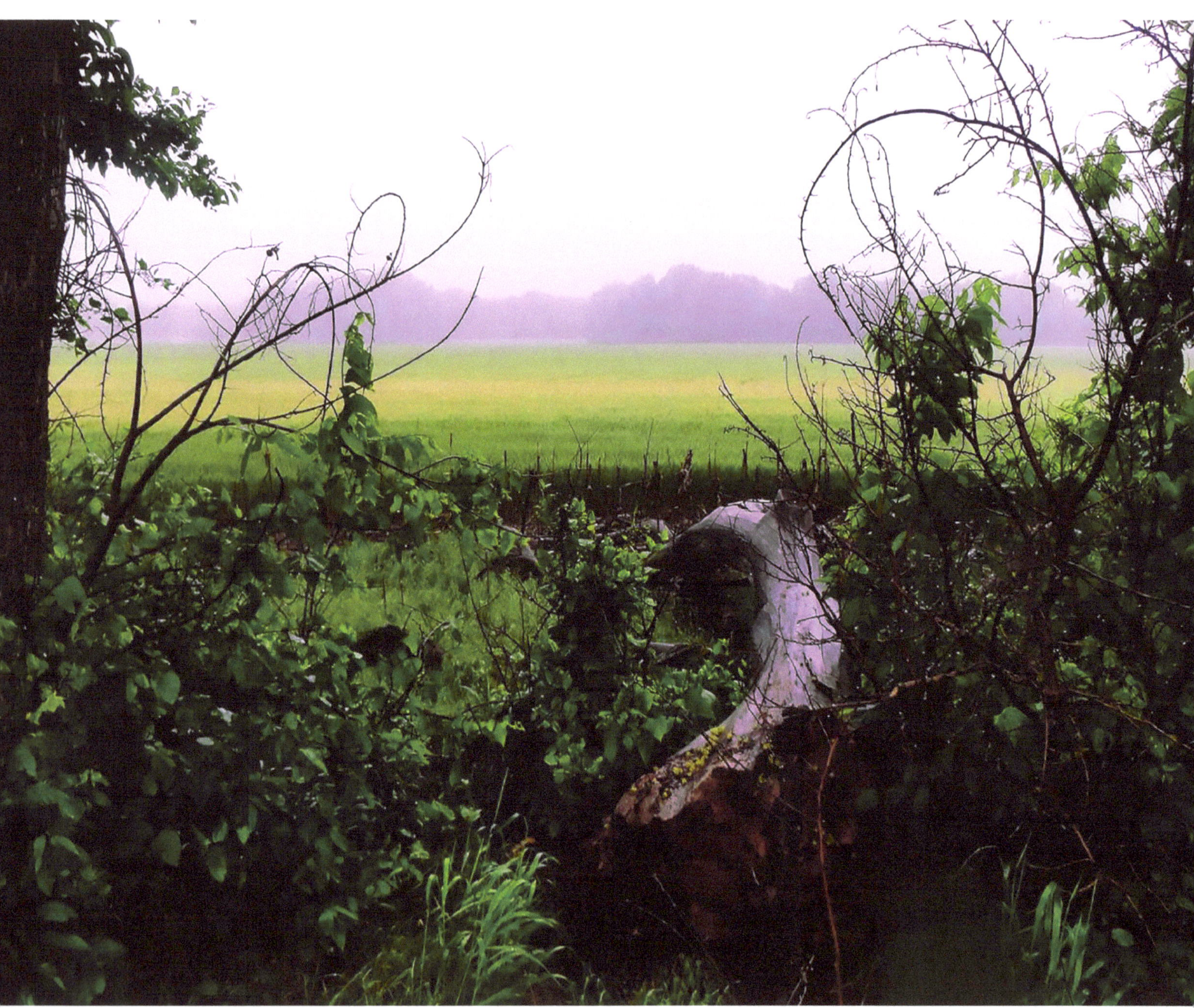

Dewey morning, Kansas (Mark Pendergrass)

These thoughts—and more—I hold in store

As fresh as dew on April's grass

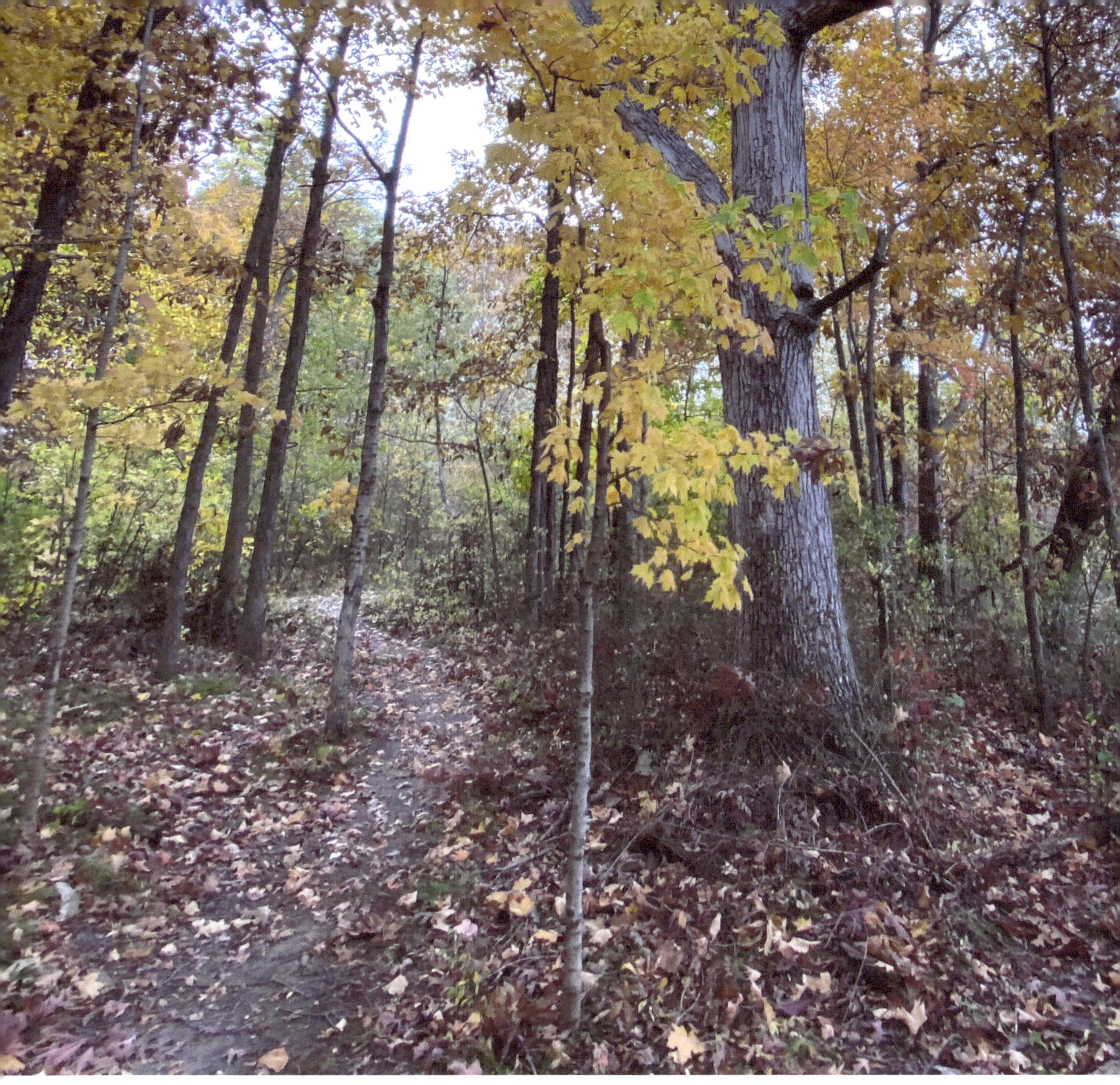

Footpath (Mark Murphy)

That lined the footpaths daily trod
By childish feet en route to class.

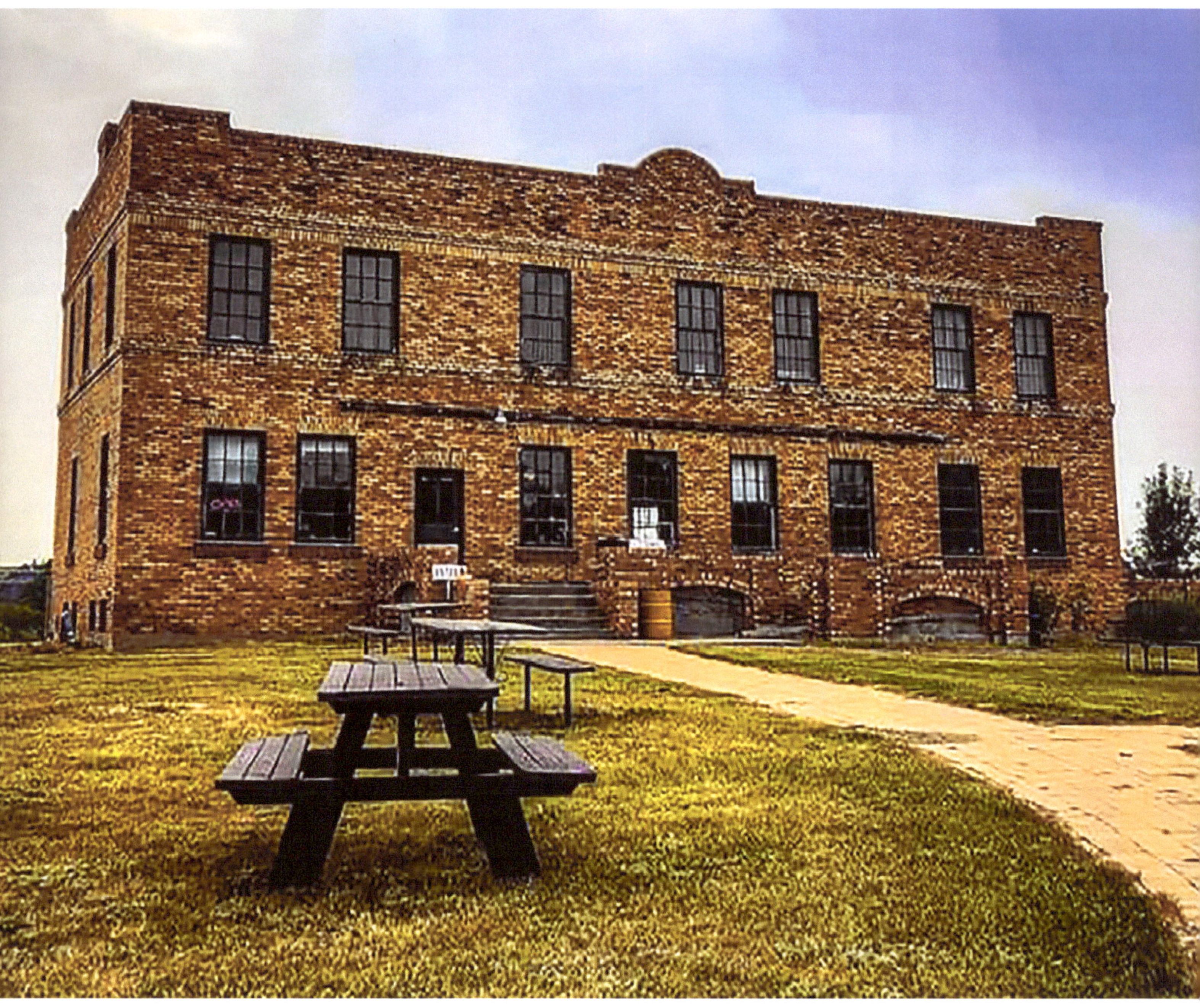

High School, Saskatchewan (Cris Sia Moresca)

The church and high school in our town
Then followed in their proper time,

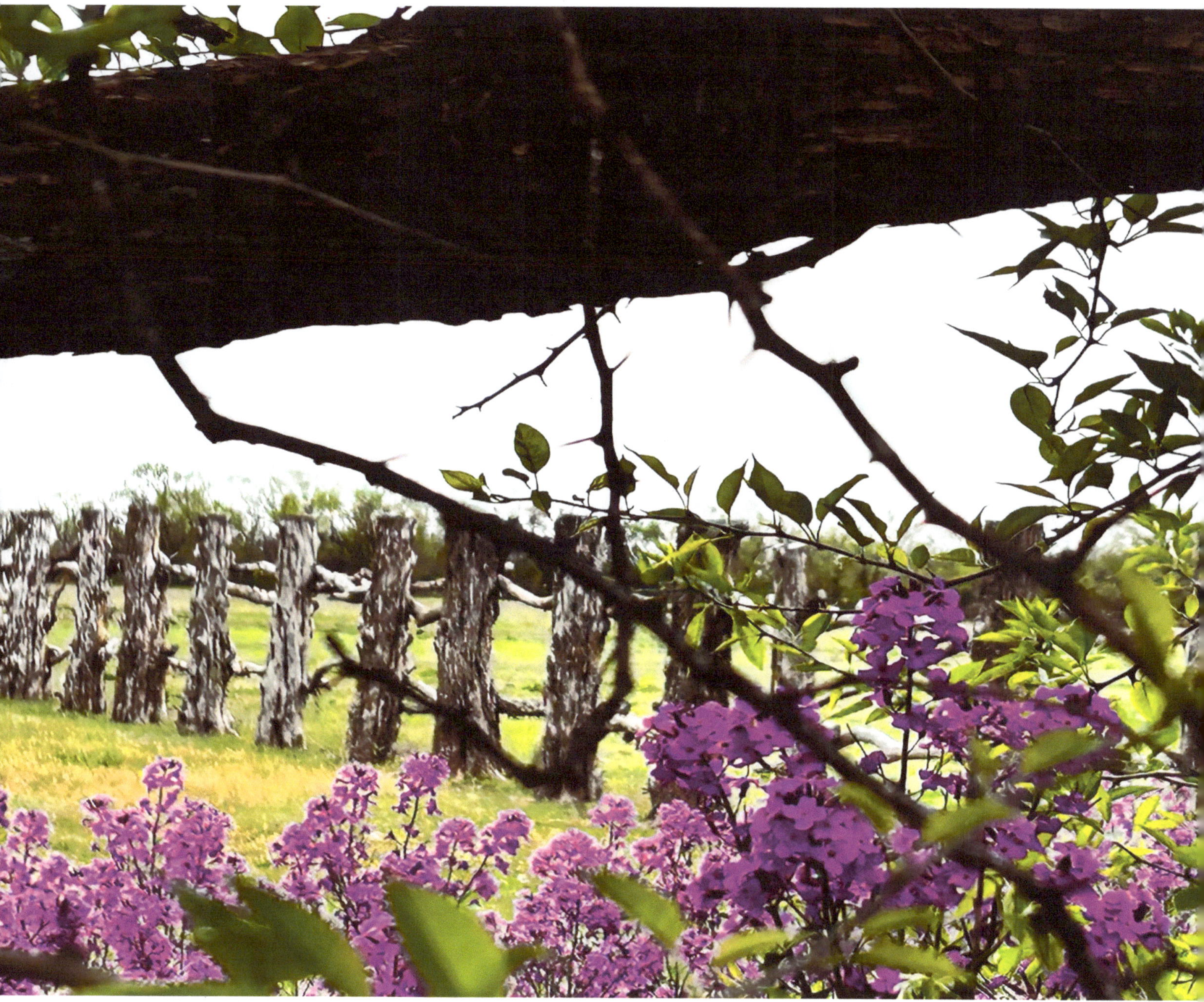

Fence and flowers, Kansas (Mark Pendergrass)

And youthful friendships thus were formed
To flourish in that Ozark clime.

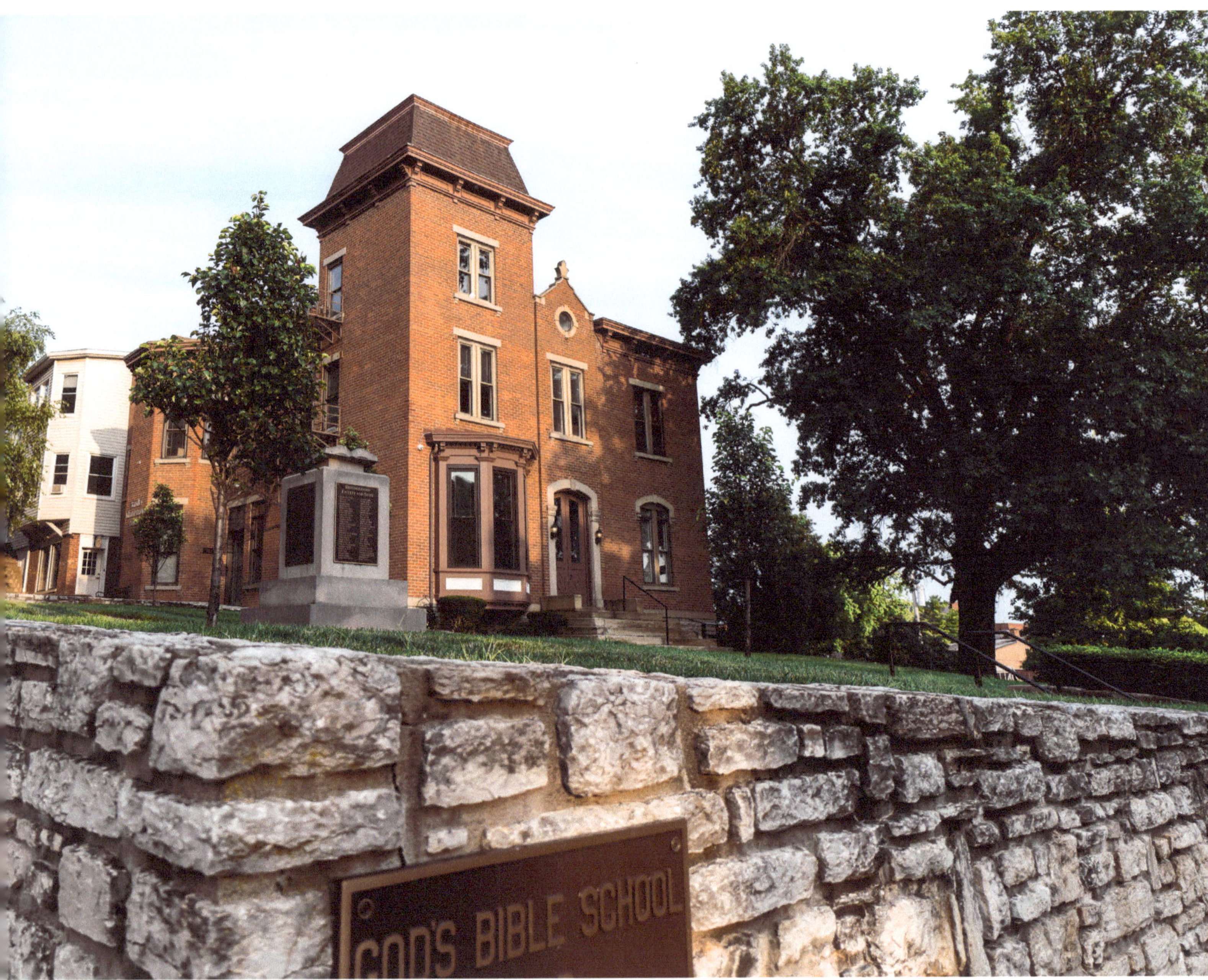

God's Bible School & College, Cincinnati

Of course, with college and career
Came still more faces and locations.

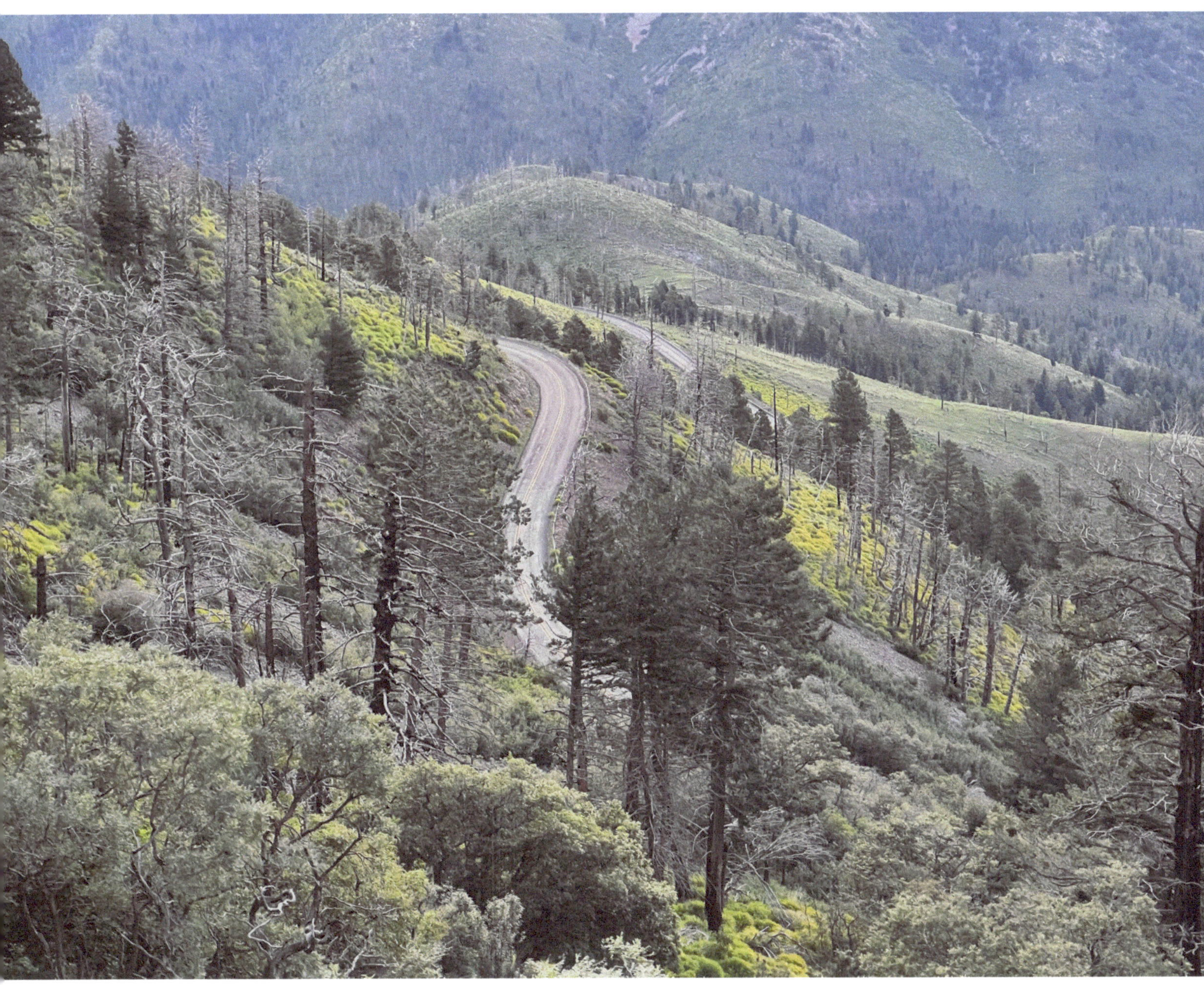

Winding mountain road (Mark Murphy)

Each move has added to my hoard
Of wondrous friends and situations.

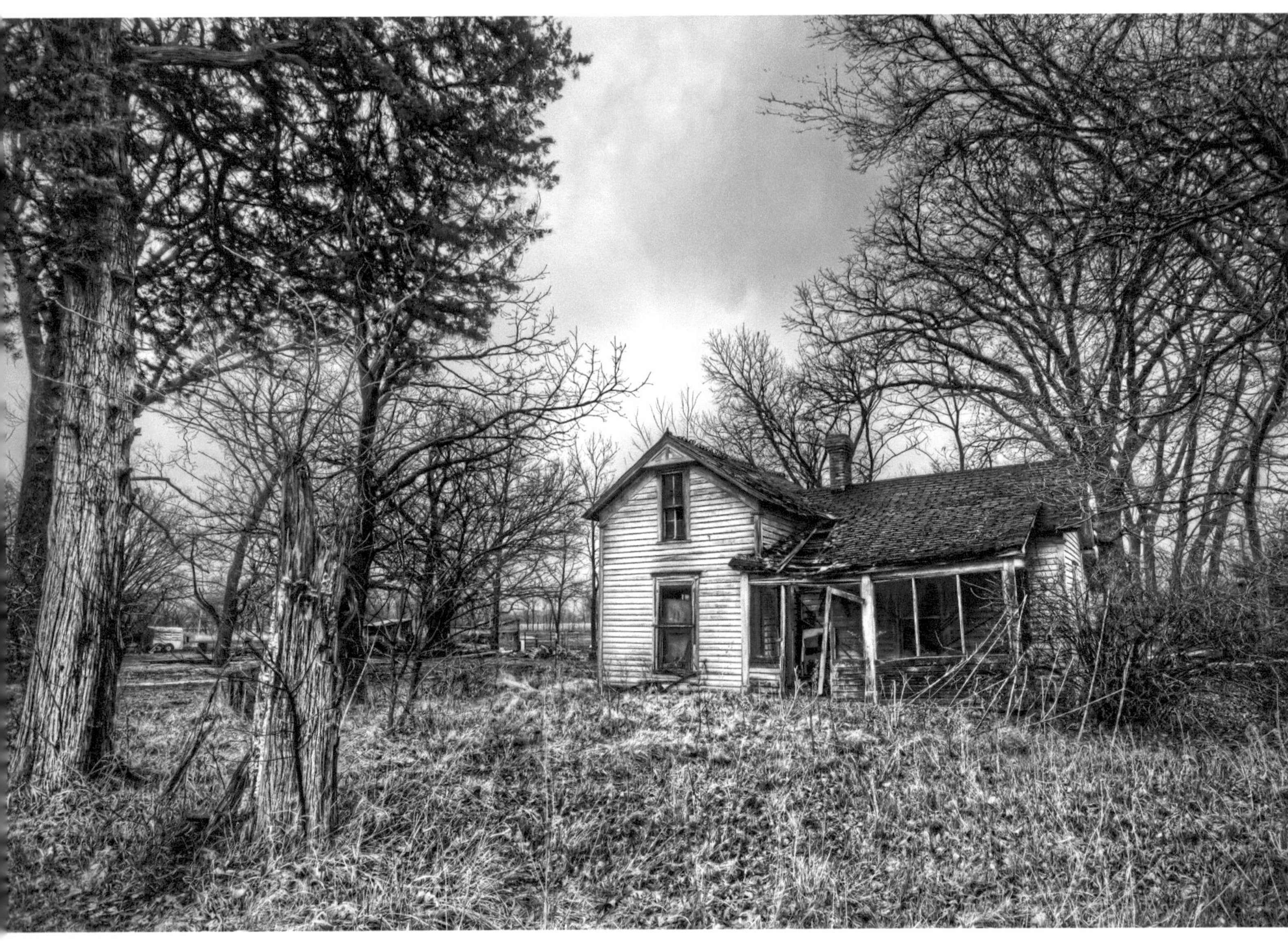

Ghost house, Florence #3, Kansas (Dave McKane)

But time moves on and, with it, people;
Closest ties must come untied.

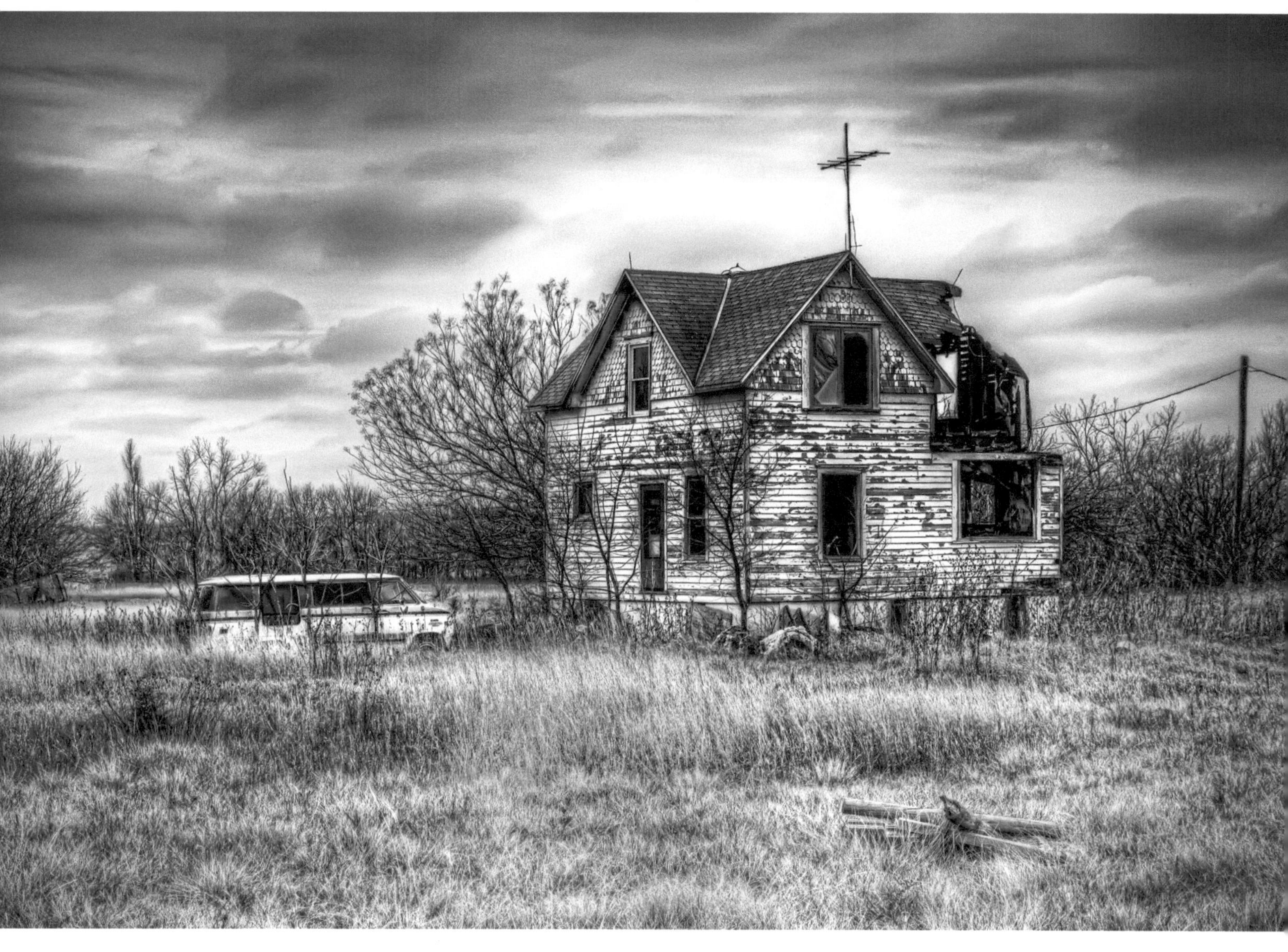

Ghost house, Lindsborg, Kansas (Dave McKane)

Our parents dear, our neighbors near
Are mem'ries on life's ebbing tide.

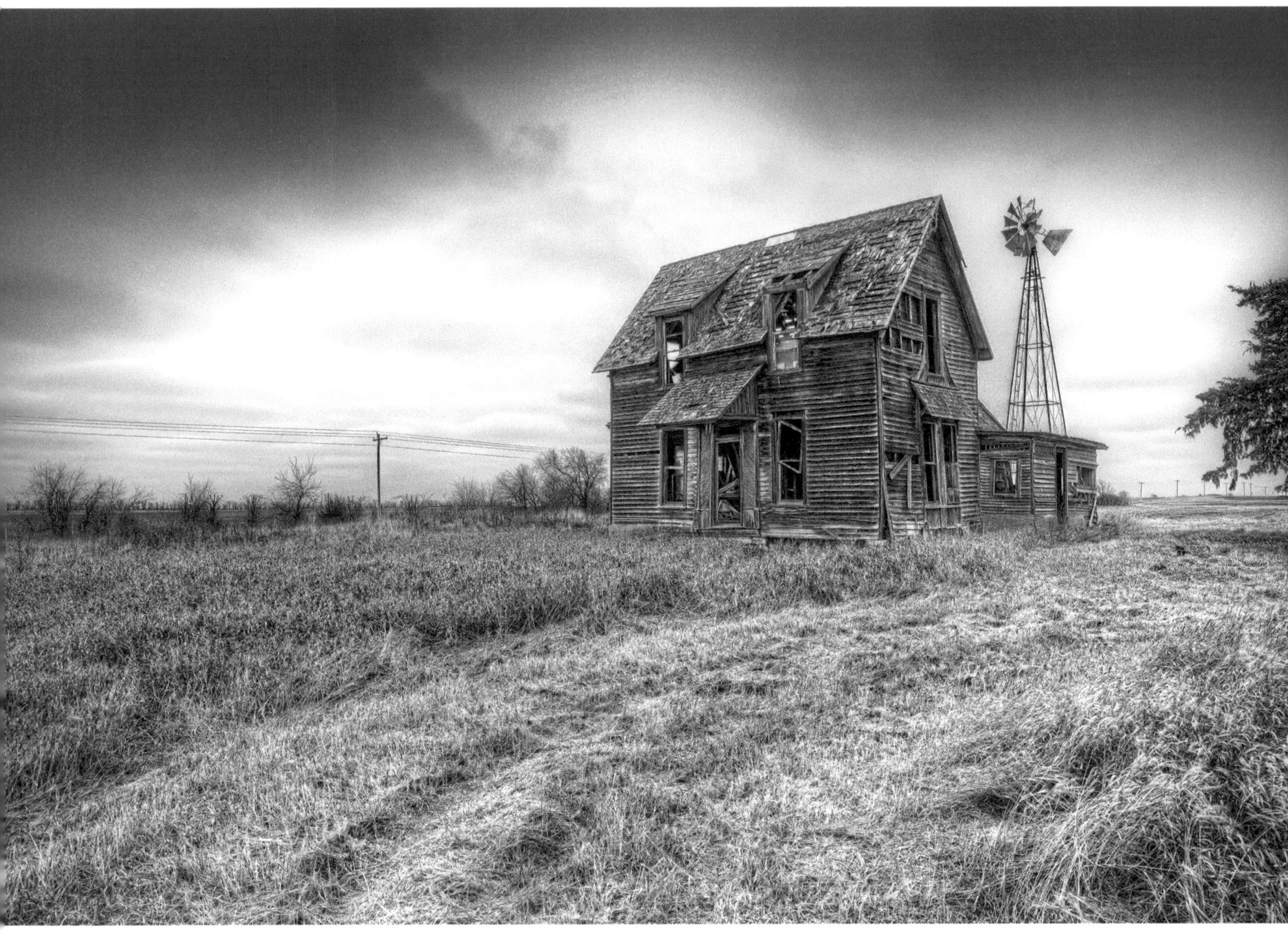

Ghost house, Lyons, Kansas (Dave McKane)

How precious are those tender thoughts
That hark us back to days gone by;

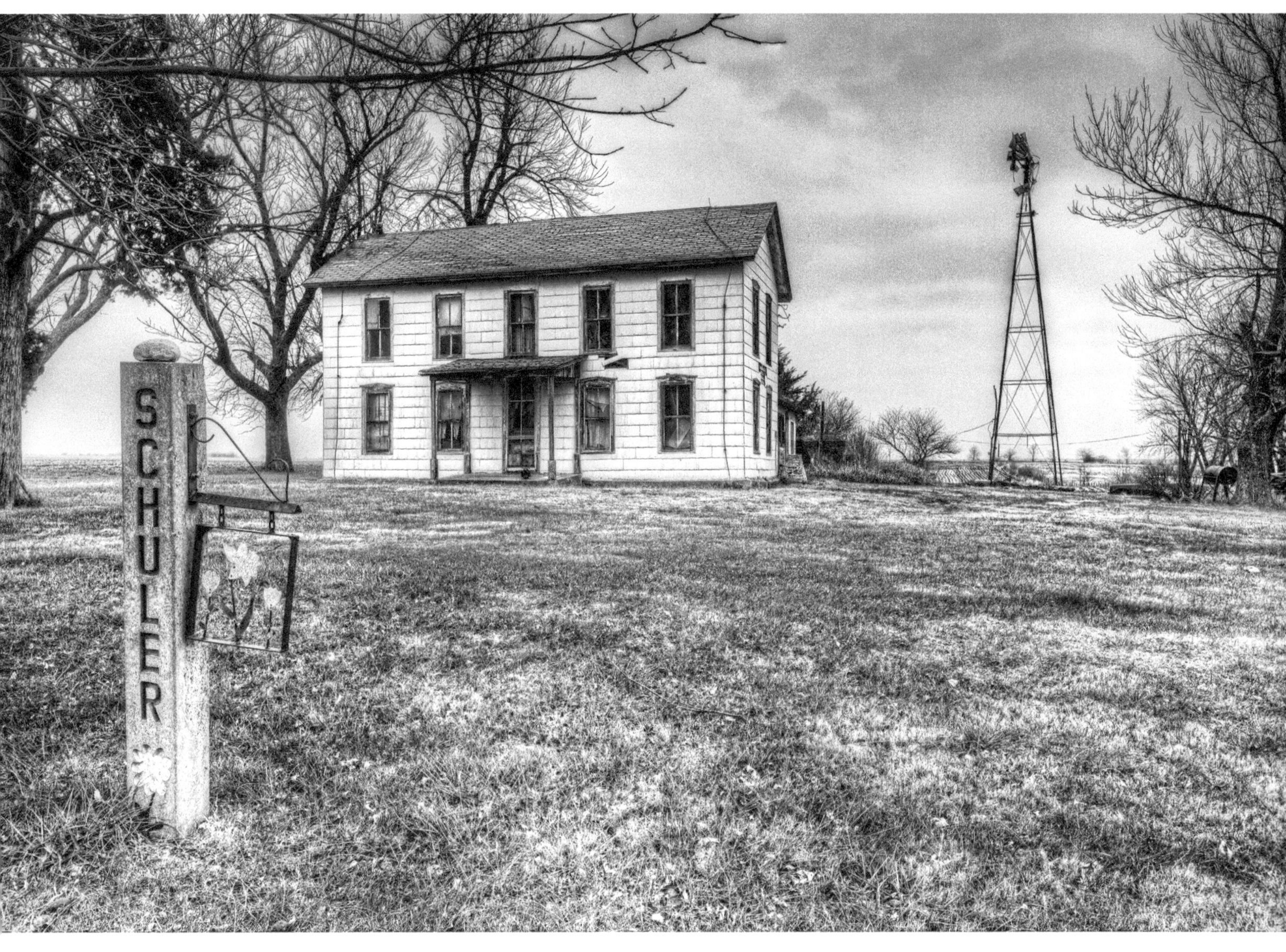

Ghost house, Nortonville, Kansas (Dave McKane)

But we can't live in yesteryear,
Nor do I think it wise to try.

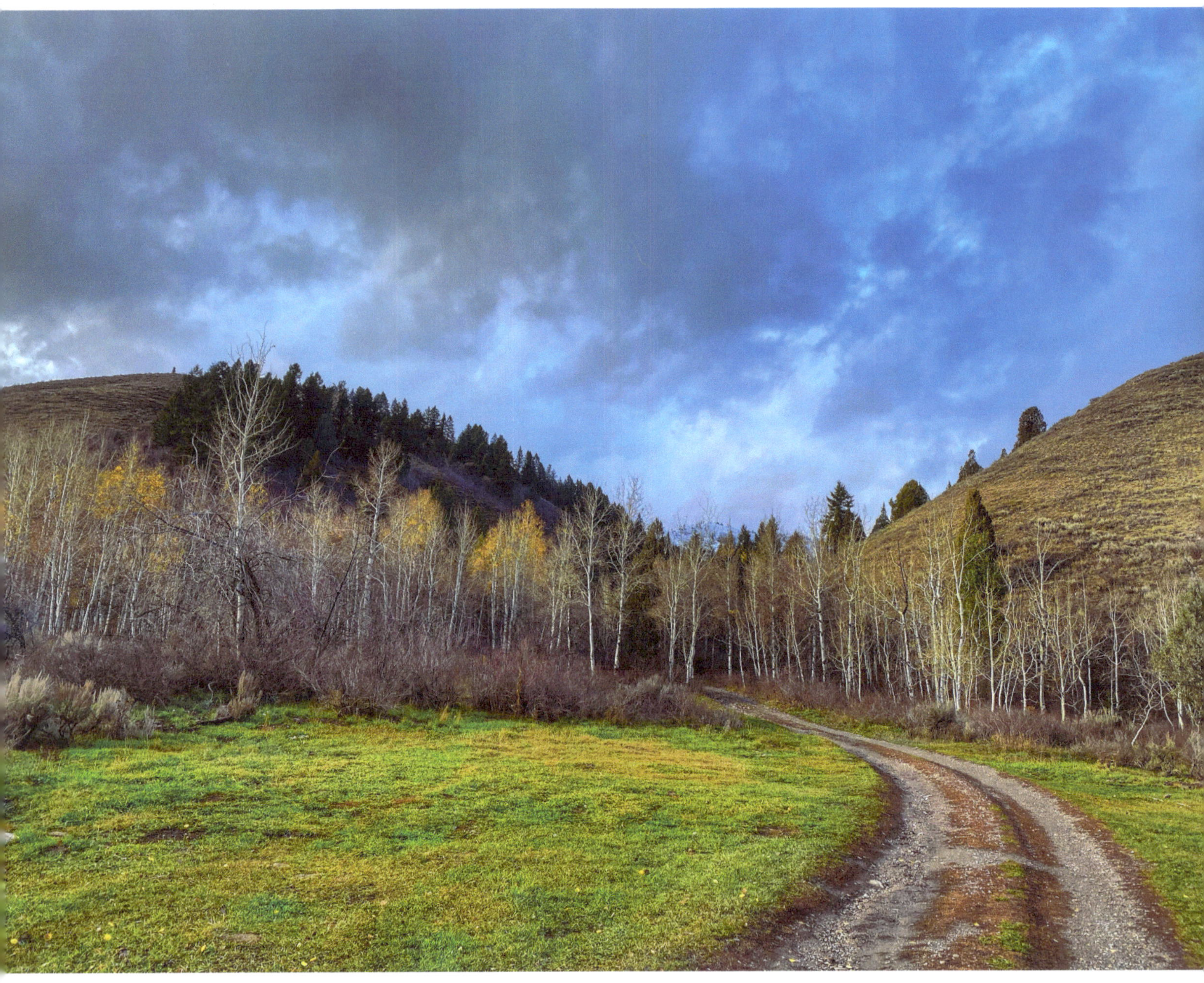

Mountain trail (Mark Murphy)

However, let me, now and then,
Revisit trails o'er which I've passed:

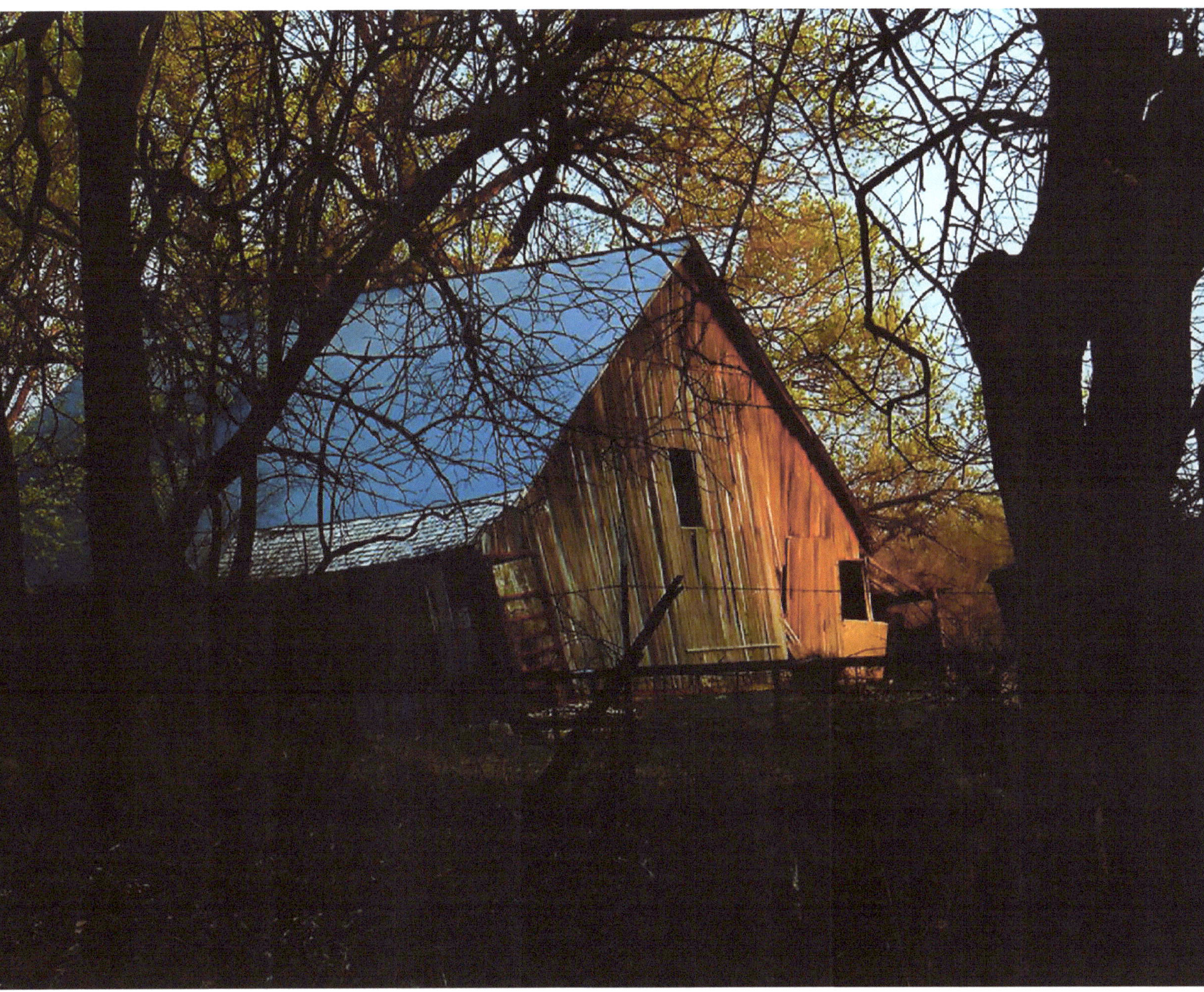

Sunset on barn, Kansas (Mark Pendergrass)

The lessons learned, the friends I've known,
Regrets and triumphs of the past.

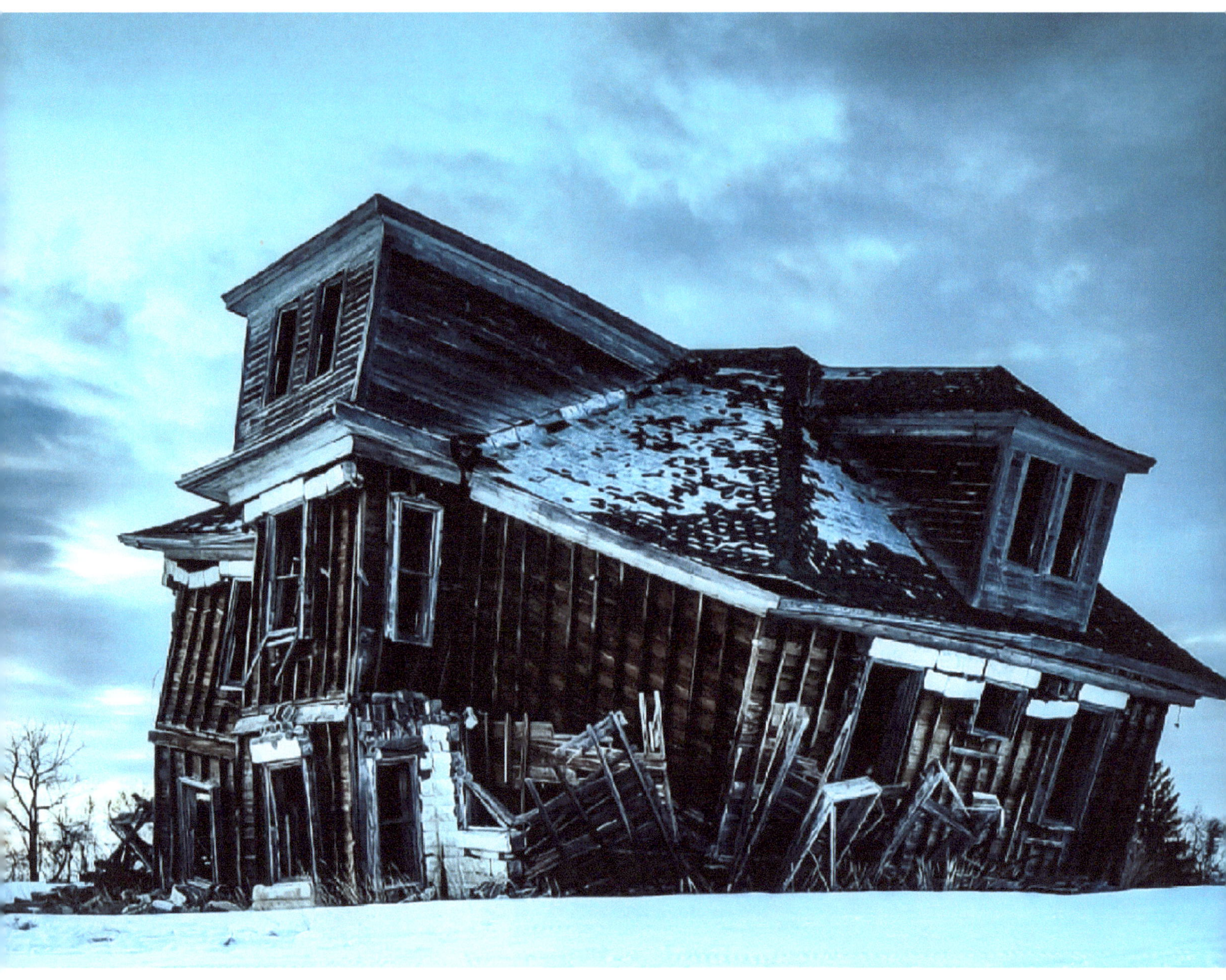

Collapsing house, Saskatchewan (Cris Sia Moresca)

I cannot slow the flight of years;

But may they never steal from me

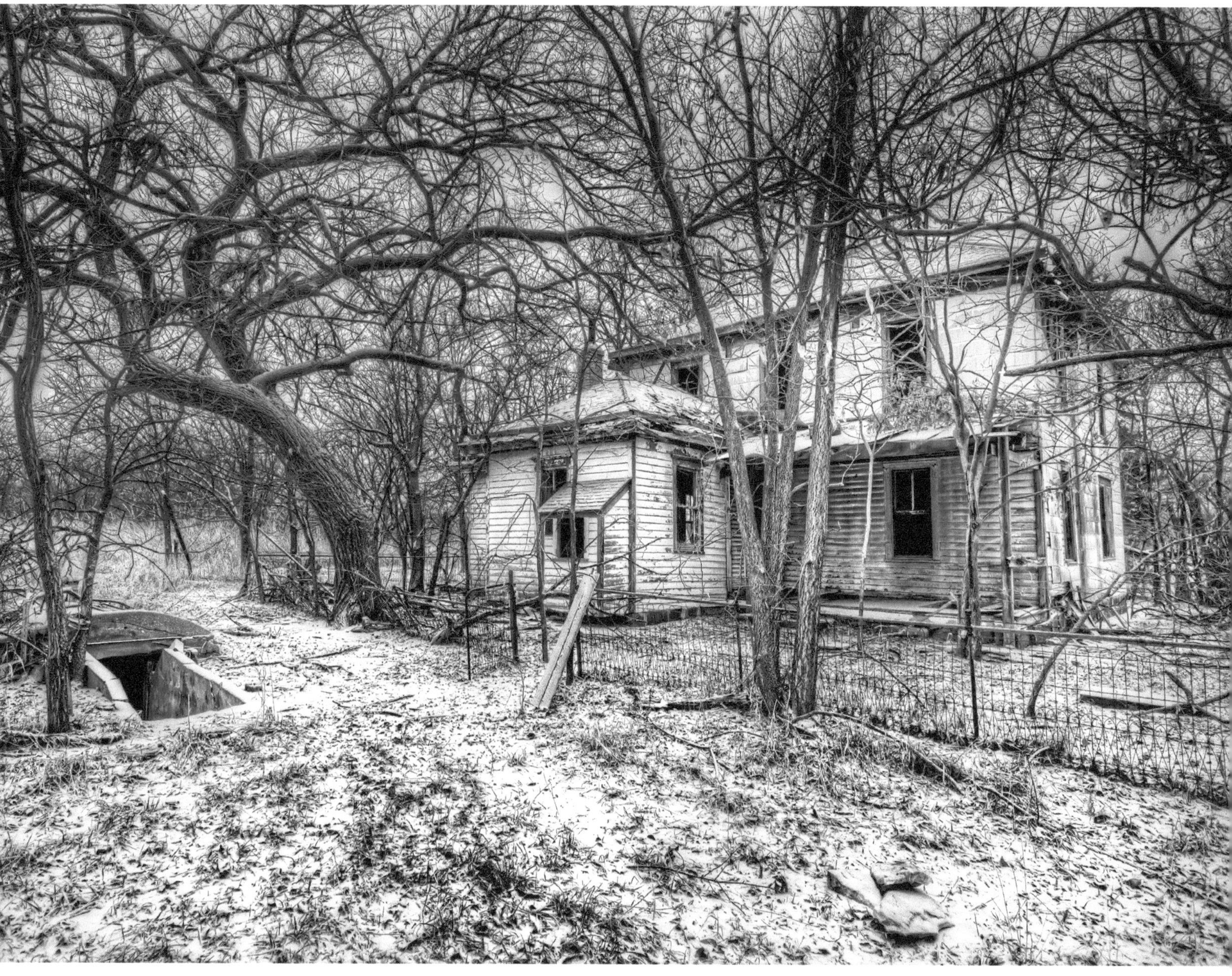

Ghost house, Falun, Kansas (Dave McKane)

Those priceless treasures that I keep
So closely held in memory.

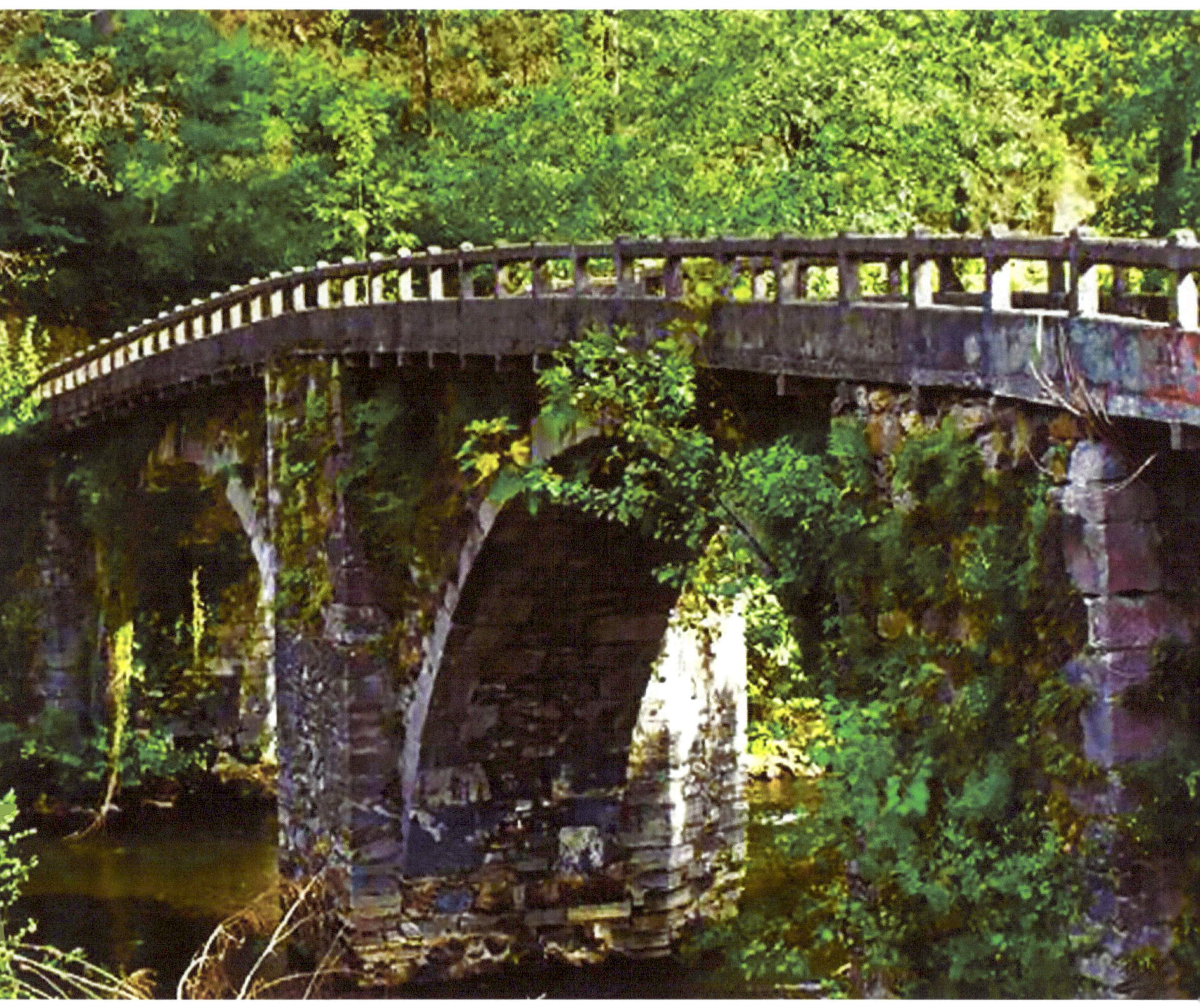

Bridge, Kansas (Mark Pendergrass)

For, living in these changing times,
I need stability, you see—

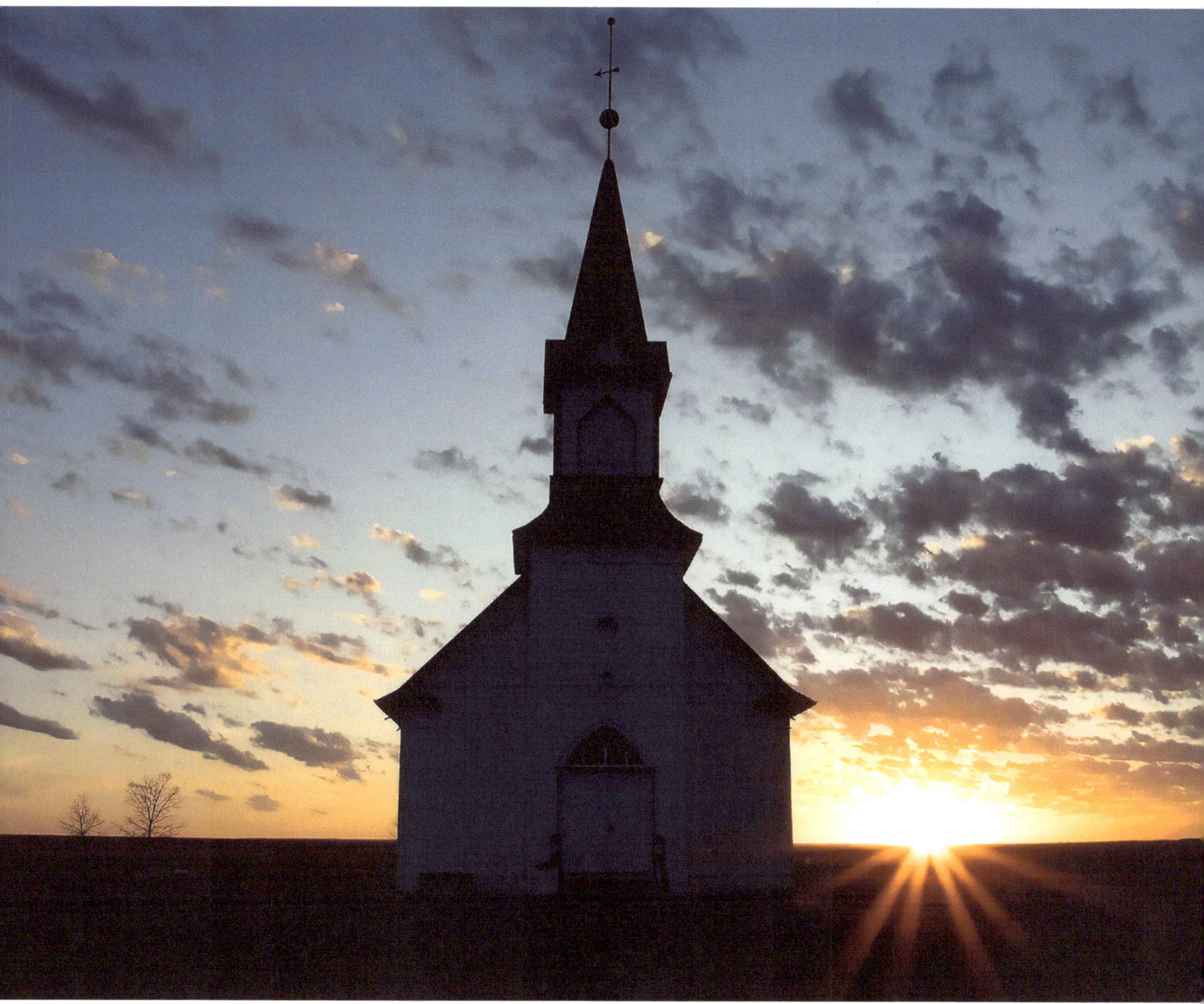

Church in sunset, Saskatchewan (Cris Sia Moresca)

A point of reference, if you please,
To hold my course unswervingly.

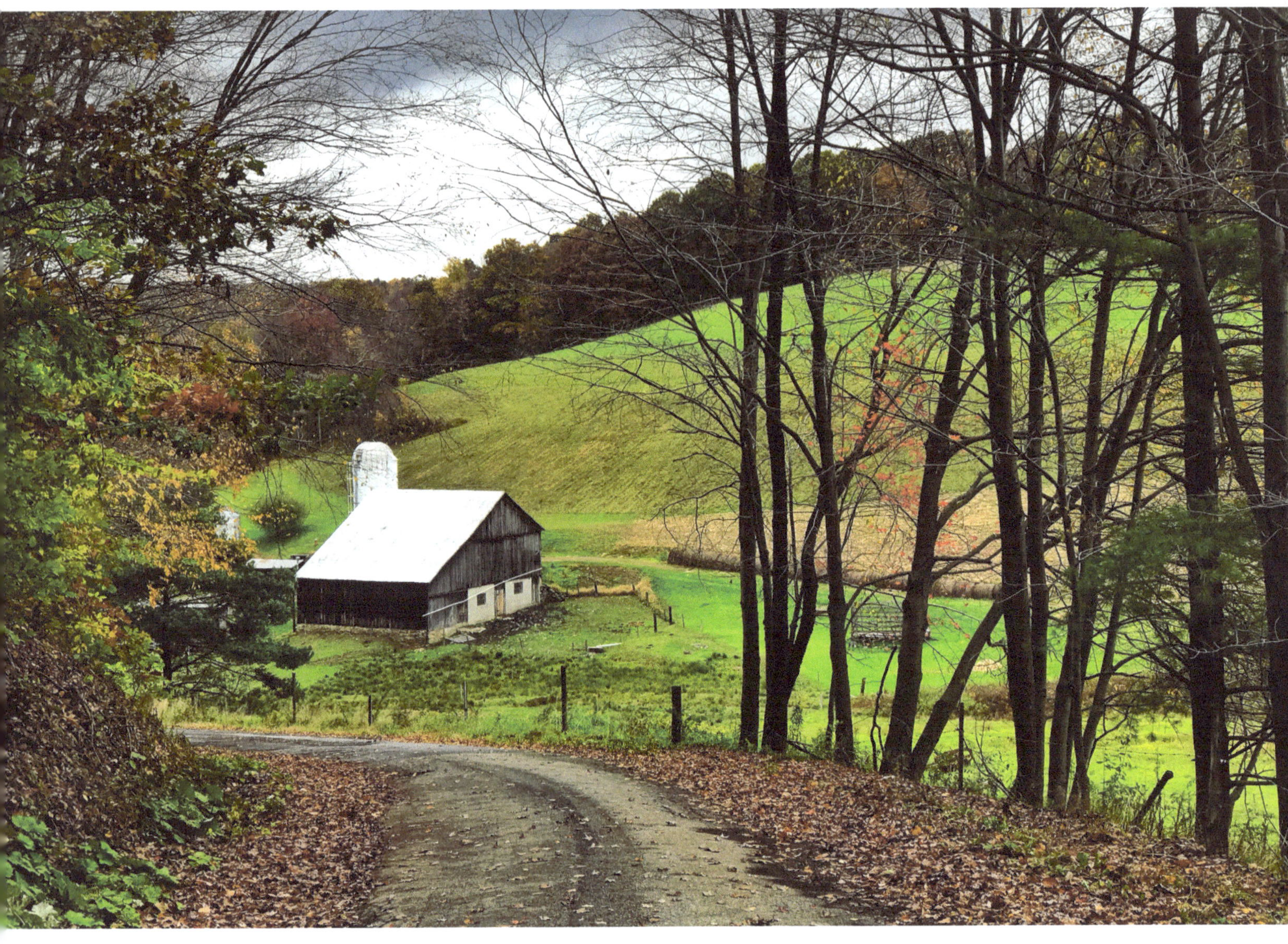

Barn in valley (Mark Murphy)

My home and friends and values found,
The faith I gained 'mongst humble folks:

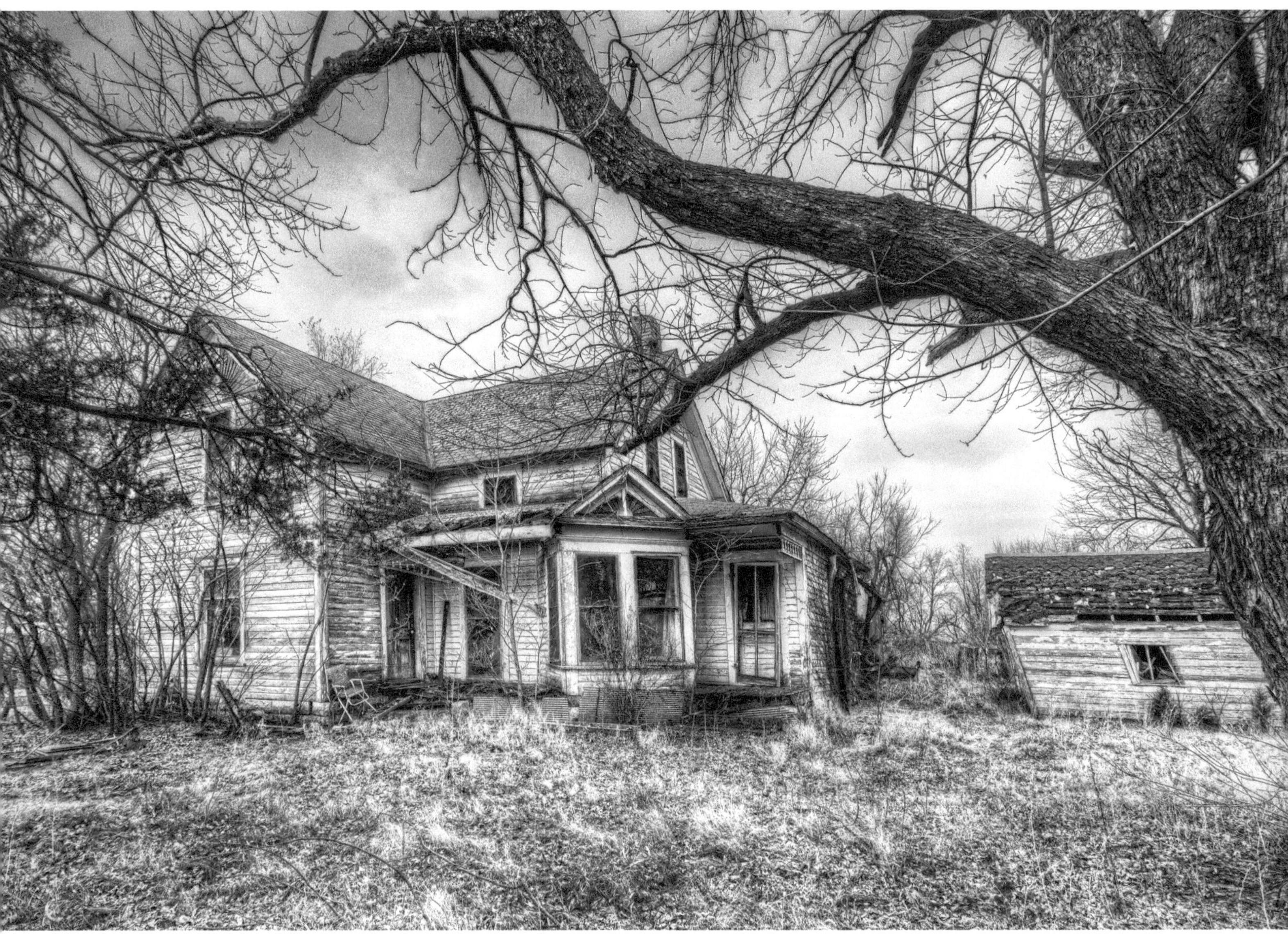

Ghost house, Hiawatha, Kansas (Dave McKane)

These act as anchor and support
Like roots to stalwart, ancient oaks.

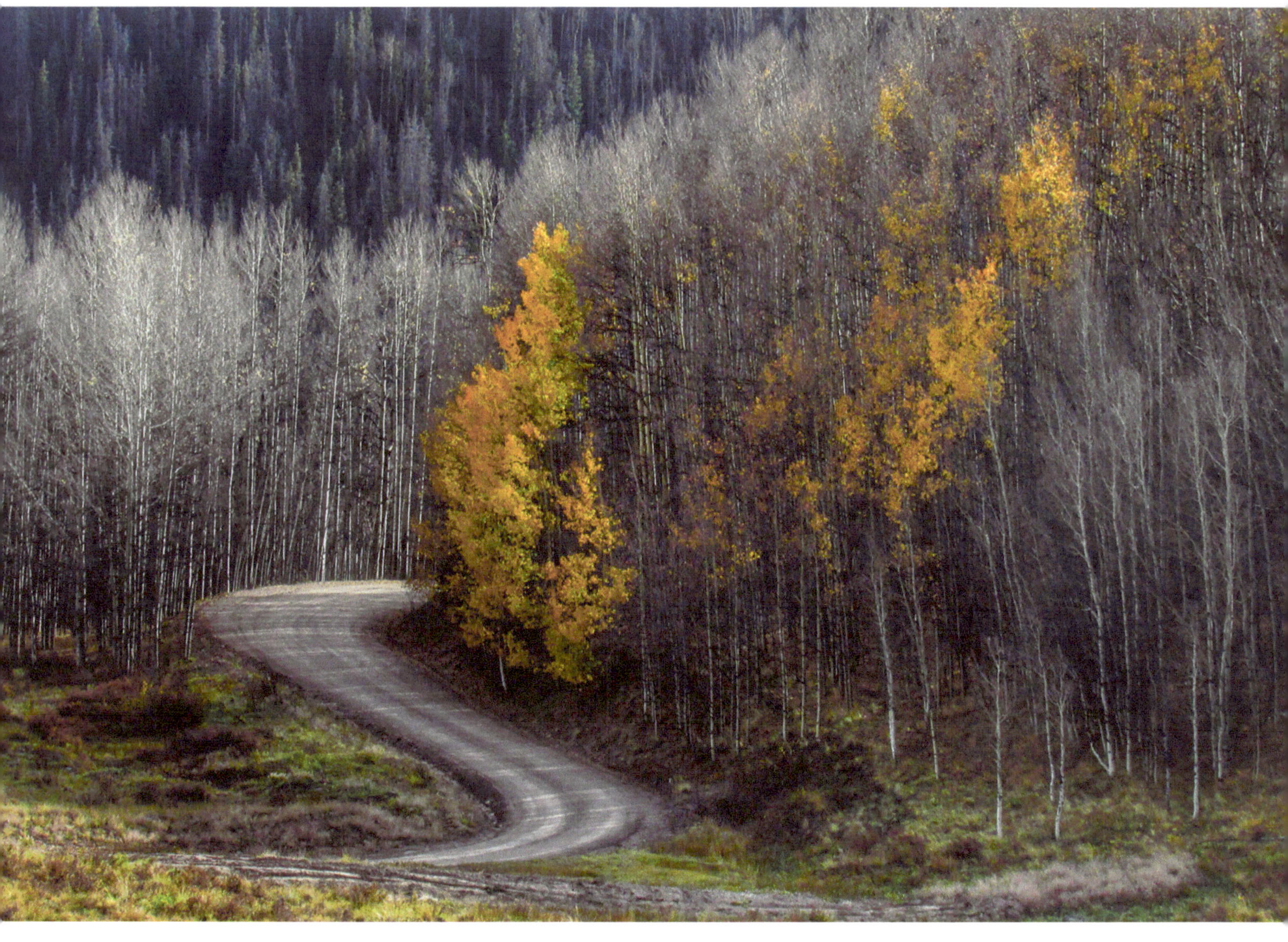

Mountain road (Mark Murphy)

Though I may journey far afield
And earn both wealth and honest praise,

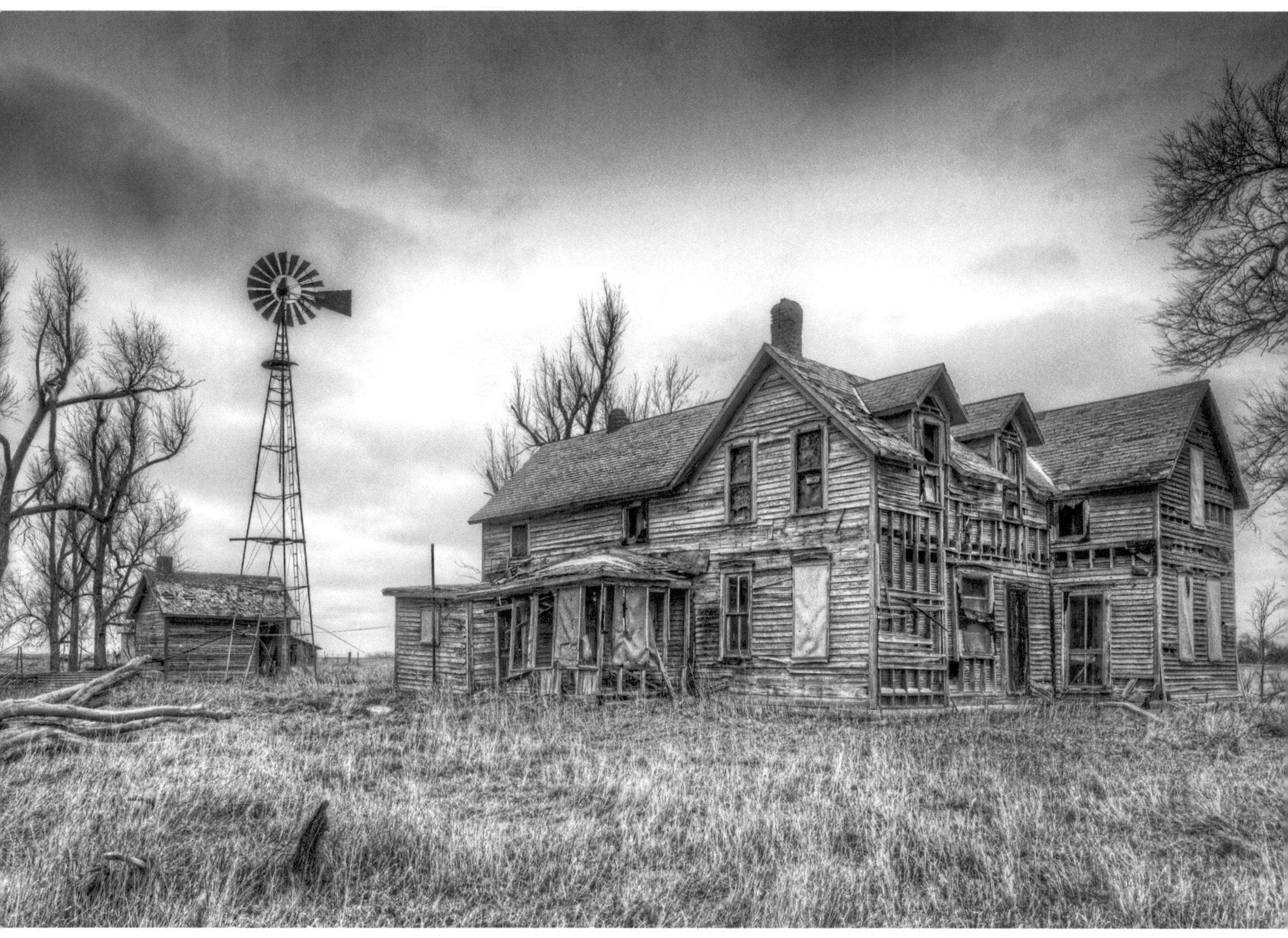

Ghost house, Pollard, Kansas (Dave McKane)

My fondest memories shall be
Of erstwhile friends and simpler days.

Acknowledgements

I wish to convey my sincere gratitude to these men and women who graciously supplied the photographs in this book:

Dave McKane, an Irishman who first noticed what he calls "ghost houses" when—as a high schooler—he was a foreign exchange student in Hutchinson, Kansas years ago. Since then he has made many trips back to the US. He writes:

The shots were taken from 2009 until 2013, although the bulk of them were done by 2011. Kansas means so much to me that it makes me want to be an integral part of that place. I think it is true to say that without my Kansas experience, and the deep validation it gave me, I would not be here today.

The primary goal was to, in a way, insert myself into Kansas history by documenting these buildings that were withering away to oblivion, bringing with them a key visual clue to the past and to the people who settled there all those decades ago.

I subsequently began to realize that I was really photographing my own family dysfunction. These ghosts of the prairies are clear evidence of a major economic catastrophe in the lives of the families who once lived there. The houses my own parents lived in, and subsequently those of my siblings, betray no such calamity, yet what goes on inside their four walls is a major emotional disaster. This sadness is essentially what drove the look and feel of the shots. I only shot them in winter, and only on very cloudy days, as a way to project even more heartache onto already poignant scenes.

As to a few words about myself, other than how important Kansas remains to me? I guess I'm someone who's drawn to creative expression as a method of both surviving and understanding life and its myriad ways of encumbering someone who has a natural tendency to think deeply. As such I rarely make money from my creative efforts as the act of creation is payment enough.

If you wish to contact Dave, you may e-mail him at dmkfinearts@gmail.com or visit his website: www.dmkfinearts.com

Mary Chew, who lives with her husband on a picturesque farm in the middle of a large Amish community in southern Missouri, and who—not coincidentally—happens to be one of my awesome sisters-in-law. When she isn't caring for animals or crops (sunflowers and pumpkins mostly), she can often be found in her artist's cottage—named Little Lavender Art Shed, which was previously an Amish tack shop.

Cris Sia Moresca, Avonlea, Saskatchewan-based amateur photographer with a passion for traveling the province's rural areas, capturing breathtaking landscapes and historic structures. Photography serves as a therapeutic outlet for this mother of two, allowing her to express her creativity while exploring new destinations and techniques. As her skills and love for photography grow, so does her appreciation for the art form.

To see more of Cris's photos, check out her Facebook business page: Click and Go (When in Saskatchewan): https://www.facebook.com/profile.php?id=100090805233286

. . . or follow Cris on Facebook: https://www.facebook.com/echit101

Click and Go

Check out my page

Cris Sia Moresca

Follow me on facebook

Mark Norman Murphy, a stage 4 colon cancer survivor, who lives near Muncie, Indiana with his wife Julie. He has traveled in almost every state in the US as well as the United Kingdom, eastern Africa, the eastern and western Caribbeans, Canada, and Mexico. Regarding his photography, Mark writes:

> The Creator created such beauty in this world, and I'm driven and honored to capture that beauty through the lens of my camera for all to enjoy.

Mark can be reached via e-mail at nmurf5@aol.com or through Facebook: https://www.facebook.com/mark.n.murphy.5

Mark D. Pendergrass, a real "renaissance man" living in Kansas: novelist, artist, early CCM producer (perhaps best known for his song "The Greatest Thing"), and influential social media content producer/commenter. Through Facebook I learned that he shared my fascination with abandoned farms, and had even written a song on the subject . . . recorded simply, at his kitchen table. His wife Rhandi added video so it could be posted to YouTube, and they graciously allowed me to share it here since it so perfectly summarizes the sentiments of this book. Aim your camera at this QR code . . .

. . . or type this into your browser:

https://www.youtube.com/watch?v=EwFMJlZyonQ (and remember that Mark has no control over the advertisement that appears at the beginning, which you can skip after 5 seconds).

Thanks, artistic friends! Dad would have loved your visual enhancements of his poems.

Lyndell Leatherman

www.ingramcontent.com/pod-product-compliance
Lightning Source LLC
Chambersburg PA
CBHW042110030726
47599CB00002B/167